UNITED STATES CRYPTOLOGIC HISTORY

Series IV
World War II
Volume 6

Pearl Harbor Revisited:
United States Navy Communications Intelligence
1924 – 1941

Frederick D. Parker

D1605075

CENTER FOR CRYPTOLOGIC HISTORY

NATIONAL SECURITY AGENCY

1994

Table of Contents

Foreword

Mr. Parker's monograph is the first in a series treating the U.S. Navy's communications intelligence (COMINT) efforts in the Pacific during World War II. A second volume (*A Priceless Advantage: U.S. Navy Communications Intelligence and the Battles of Coral Sea, Midway, and the Aleutians*), was recently published.

The series as a whole and this volume in particular are unique in many ways but primarily because they represent a closely analyzed, comprehensive examination of the COMINT record juxtaposed with extensive research into the written history of events. Mr. Parker's work also includes research into the Japanese Navy messages which remained untranslated until 1945 and undiscovered until now. These messages revealed the Japanese Navy plans for war with the United States, Great Britain, and the Netherlands and the preliminary exercises which occurred in the months prior to Pearl Harbor. This activity clearly signaled the creation of a massive carrier strike force with the major naval objective somewhere in the Pacific Ocean far distant from either Indochina or the Philippines.

This comparison of the COMINT record with the published material covering the same period will benefit not only NSA but the academic community, which continues to pursue the history of the Second World War. Thus whether or not the results agree with the literature, particularly if they do not, the effort to create an "official" COMINT history is more than justified.

Mr. Parker's perseverance, diligent research, and detailed analysis have made this a significant and unique contribution to U.S. COMINT history, U.S. military history, and U.S. history.

Henry F. Schorreck
NSA Historian (Ret.)

Pearl Harbor Revisited:
United States Navy Communications Intelligence
1924 – 1941

"The aspect of the Pearl Harbor disaster which is really surprising is that so many people failed to do either the obvious or the sensible things." Washington Star, 1 September 1945

INTRODUCTION

This is the story of the U.S. Navy's communications intelligence (COMINT) effort between 1924 and 1941. It traces the building of a program, under the Director of Naval Communications (OP-20), which extracted both radio and traffic intelligence from foreign military, commercial, and diplomatic communications.[1] It shows the development of a small but remarkable organization (OP-20-G) which, by 1937, could clearly see the military, political, and even the international implications of effective cryptography and successful cryptanalysis at a time when radio communications were passing from infancy to childhood and Navy war planning was restricted to tactical situations.[2] It also illustrates an organization plagued from its inception by shortages in money, manpower, and equipment, total absence of a secure, dedicated communications system, little real support or tasking from higher command authorities, and major imbalances between collection and processing capabilities. It explains how, in 1941, as a result of these problems, compounded by the stresses and exigencies of the time, the effort misplaced its **focus from Japanese Navy traffic to Japanese diplomatic messages. Had Navy** cryptanalysts been ordered to concentrate on the Japanese naval messages rather than Japanese diplomatic traffic, the United States would have had a much clearer picture of the Japanese military buildup and, with the warning provided by these messages, might have avoided the disaster of Pearl Harbor.

This story also records what today must be ranked as an intensely important interlude when the Navy radio/traffic intelligence program deliberately avoided the underlying intelligence of intercepted traffic while exploiting foreign cryptographic systems. Today most intelligence experts would call such a practice naive or ill advised. Yet a policy requiring OP-20-G cryptanalysts to search primarily for unique cryptographic features of codes and ciphers which might later be refined and employed by Navy cryptographers was not changed until 1942. Coupled with a reluctance to hire civilian trainees, this policy seriously delayed the training of enough Navy cryptanalysts and linguists to deal with a work load which increased exponentially both in complexity and volume after 1939. Ultimately, the resulting shortage of cryptanalysts and Japanese linguists, the problem of misplaced priorities, and interservice rivalry issues all contributed to misplacing the major focus of the Navy's cryptanalytic and linguistic efforts on Japanese diplomatic messages. The unfortunate result of these circumstances was to postpone with fatal consequences an all-out effort on Japanese Navy cryptosystems.

This is not to minimize the value of the pre-Pearl Harbor efforts of Navy cryptanalysts and traffic analysts. Even without the messages pertaining to the Japanese Pearl Harbor strike force, the magnitude of the information they produced pertaining to the Japanese 2nd, 3rd and 4th Fleets and the Japanese 11th Air Fleet was overwhelming. These intimate details concerning Japanese intentions, however, were not based on messages but on analytic judgments drawn from analysis of Japanese Navy communications procedures, patterns, and practices. As suspect quantities from a suspect source, they were not accepted by the very commanders in whose service they had been developed. The lack of confidence in such intelligence made traffic intelligence from the Pacific during the last half of 1941 more an elaborate rumor than trustworthy source material. Commanders at the theater level and in Washington, through lack of early training or insight, were not prepared to exploit the intelligence provided by this source, particularly when the messages themselves could not be read.

In addition to outlining the development of the Navy's cryptanalytic attack against Japanese cryptographic systems, this review also examines other interesting episodes overseas and in Washington which included two attempts, one unsuccessful, to coordinate Navy and Army COMINT activities, efforts to improve fleet communications, and the lessons learned and then forgotten about Japanese naval communications from Japanese Fleet maneuvers of the 1930s. Coordination and cooperation between the U.S. Navy COMINT Center on Corregidor and the British Far East Combined Bureau in Singapore are briefly described.

EARLIEST EFFORTS

The origins of the U.S. Navy's COMINT effort prior to 1924 are not entirely clear. However, the Navy established a Code and Signal Section possibly with COMINT interests as early as 28 July 1916. This small organization initially worked against German ciphers during World War I. It also tested the security of U.S. Navy ship-to-ship and ship-to-shore communications during training maneuvers. During the maneuvers of 1917, for example, personnel from the section were involved in an overt attempt to intercept and exploit U.S. Navy communications in order to demonstrate their accessibility to foreign intelligence efforts.[3]

For some unknown reason, these initiatives apparently ended with the World War in 1918. At that time the Navy voluntarily consolidated its wartime efforts with those of the War, Justice, State, and Postal Censorship Departments, forming a single U.S. Cipher Bureau under the War Department. Commanded by Captain Herbert O. Yardley, assisted by Captain John W. Manly, the consolidated bureau consisted of thirteen cryptographers, twelve of whom were women, and an administrator. It was supported by eleven student officers, eight stenographers, and fifteen clerks. The Navy was represented by Chief Yeoman H. E. Burt.[4]

From 1919 to 1923 the Navy seemed to rely almost entirely on the Cipher Bureau. In 1923 the Navy apparently felt that the Cipher Bureau had produced neither the desired cryptographic improvements nor the necessary insights into the activities of foreign navies, in particular Japan's growing fleet. Accordingly, using shipboard communicators, the U.S. Navy in 1923 began an ad hoc effort to listen to foreign radio traffic, which its earlier work had shown to be potentially vulnerable to penetration and exploitation.

In January 1924, Commander Ridley McClean, Director of Naval Communication (DNC) established a research desk within the Code and Signal Section with a complement of one officer, Lieutenant Laurance F. Safford, and one civilian, Agnes Meyer, both of whom were cryptanalysts/cryptographers. Safford and Meyer conducted research into foreign cryptography, organized training in collection and cryptanalysis, developed cryptographic systems for naval communications, and arranged with the Commander in Chief, Asiatic Fleet (CINCAF), and certain naval district commanders to obtain copies of radio intercept of foreign messages. The primary goal of the two was to develop cryptographic systems for the U.S. Navy which would avoid the weaknesses observed in the cryptographic techniques employed by foreign governments.

Before tackling the problems of penetration and exploitation on a regular basis, the Navy had to construct an organization which could routinely intercept and process foreign cryptographic systems. Beginning as a totally decentralized effort loosely managed from Washington, D.C., collection and local exploitation of plain text was controlled by fleet and naval district commanders, while Washington retained control of the cryptanalytic capability.

Early in 1924, Commander McClean, and the Chief of Naval Operations (CNO), Admiral Edward W. Eberle, encouraged the Commander in Chief, Asiatic Fleet (CINCAF), Admiral Thomas Washington, to expand radio intelligence facilities in his area. As a result of this encouragement, the first Navy intercept station ashore (Station A) was established the same year at

Captain Laurance F. Safford

3

Shanghai in the U.S. Consulate. It copied both naval and commercial traffic (Japanese and British). Admiral Washington was responsible for all aspects of the operation including administration, logistics, personnel, and targeting. OP-20-G received all intercept logs, including traffic and messages for cryptanalysis. After the codes were broken and the messages reduced to plain text, the contents were then sent to the Office of Naval Intelligence (ONI) where, if necessary, they were translated into English.[5]

ROLE OF ONI

This decision to emphasize a communications security (COMSEC) objective in exploiting foreign communications was to prove costly to OP-20-G. It unwittingly conceded to others, notably the Office of Naval Intelligence, the responsibility for developing and disseminating underlying intelligence, control of language billets and, by thus sowing confusion regarding the nature of communications intelligence, sacrificed much of the long-term initiative regarding direction of the overall effort. The scope of ONI's COMINT-related activities and the magnitude of the cost of this concession in both human and fiscal terms can be illustrated in part by the following story. In 1930, the existence of a secret fund at Riggs Bank in Washington – at one time as large as $100,000 – administered by the Director of Naval Intelligence (DNI) accidentally came to light during the transition of ONI directors. This fund was used to buy equipment and material in support of DNC's efforts to intercept and exploit foreign radio communications. A strong possibility exists that the fund was also used to underwrite the costs of stealing, photographing, and translating the Japanese Imperial Navy Secret Operations Code (the Red Book) twice between 1921 and 1927. In 1931, over the futile objections of Captain Stanley C. Hooper, DNC, and Commander J. W. McClaran, OP-20-G, the acting Director of Naval Intelligence, Captain William Baggaley, returned the entire balance in the account ($65,000) to the U.S. Treasury. Why he did this is not clear. It may have been part of a Hoover administration economy move. Within the Navy the effects were startling. From 1931 to 1933, Admiral William V. Pratt, CNO, in retaliation for this action, ordered that ONI not be shown any of the thousands of deciphered messages available each year – a policy which must have caused extensive reassignments among ONI's Japanese linguists. In 1929 Lieutenant Commander Safford had advised Hooper that, over a five-year period, it had accumulated 10,000 Japanese diplomatic messages and, in two years, 2,000 Japanese naval messages.[6]

The early success of OP-20-G in obtaining official and commercial foreign radio traffic and exploiting the knowledge gained from decrypts made possible by acquisition of the Japanese Navy's operation code, had an immediate as well as far-reaching effect on the Navy at large. In March 1926, for example, a secret memorandum from Admiral Edward W. Eberle, CNO, to all major commands noted that current war plans did not "adequately reflect benefits gained from radio intelligence." Accordingly, Admiral Eberle directed that

4

"unit commanders both afloat and ashore . . . develop their own plans for service of radio intelligence in war." Eberle's letter also recommended (1) "intercept and decoding units" ashore and afloat; (2) direction finding (DF) units in each naval district but primarily in the 12th (Headquarters San Francisco), and in the headquarters of the Atlantic and Pacific Fleets; and (3) translators in the 14th Naval District (Hawaiian Islands) and in Washington. Clearly this represented a major change in perspective regarding radio intelligence and translators which had been inspired by the work of Station A (Shanghai), ONI, and the cryptanalysts in Washington, Safford and Meyers.

The years 1926 through 1928, however, saw little deliberate progress by the commands in implementing Eberle's desires, strongly suggesting that the message about COMINT's value was not widely accepted. Rear Admiral George R. Marvell, the Commandant 14th Naval District (COM-14), did mention radio intelligence in his 1928 war plan, but his attempts to establish an official intercept site at Wailupe, Hawaii, proved abortive. In the Asiatic Fleet area, neither Admiral Mark L. Bristol, CINCAF, nor Rear Admiral Summer E. W. Kittelle, Commandant 16th Naval District (COM-16), made any move to enlarge on Station A, although Guam and the U.S. legation at Peking began to appear in correspondence as possible candidates for new sites.

Admiral Joseph N. Wenger, USN

In the training of intercept operators and cryptanalysts, nevertheless, some real progress did occur during this period. In 1926 Ensign Joseph N. Wenger was the first officer to undergo training in a cryptanalysis "short course." Training for officers consisted of on-the-job training and semiformal instruction by Safford and Meyer. Wenger was followed in the same year by Lieutenant Joseph J. Rochefort and Captain Leo F. S. Horan, USMC. After completing his class, Rochefort was put in charge of the Research Desk while Safford performed his required sea duty. Thus Rochefort was in charge in 1926–1927 when Meyer succeeded in the initial solution of the Red Book ciphers and in discovering the "transposition forms." Later the various keys and forms used with a specific cipher were also solved by students.[7]

5

In 1928 the Navy also established a school for enlisted Navy and Marine Corps intercept operators at the Navy Department in Washington, D.C. A classroom and eight intercept positions were erected on the roof of "Main Navy" probably as much for the sake of privacy as for the lack of space. Understandably, student graduates became known as the "On the Roof Gang." The first class began on 1 October 1928. Out of twenty students in the first class, seven finished. All seven were sent to Guam to open that station in 1929.[8] Two classes, 5 and 15, were made up entirely of U.S. Marines. The school operated until February 1941. Its objective was to train carefully selected military radio operators in specialized radio communications techniques, particularly Japanese intercept, traffic analysis, and simple cryptanalysis.[9]

Encouraged by these developments, Lieutenant Commander Arthur D. Struble, OP-20-G, early in 1929, drafted a letter to Admiral Charles B. McVay, CINCAF, which directed the expansion of radio intelligence service in his command, including activities in China. Significantly, Admiral Charles F. Hughes, CNO, who signed the letter, again mentioned that "major decrypting units are planned for Washington and Honolulu."[10] Responding to this pressure from the Office of Chief of Naval Operations, McVay opened shore stations at Guam (Station B) and at the U.S. legation at Peking, and created a position on his staff for a radio intelligence officer. A special cipher was supplied to enable this officer to maintain close liaison with OP-20-G in Washington.[11] In addition, in late 1929 Rear Admiral William D. MacDougall, Commandant 16th Naval District, who was subordinate to CINCAF, opened an intercept station at a small naval base at Olongapo in the Philippines on Subic Bay facing the South China Sea. This site (Station C) was destined to move three times in ten years in an attempt to find secure operating spaces, living quarters, and antenna sites where Japanese Navy signals could be heard consistently. (Olongapo, 1930–34; Mariveles, 1934–35; Cavite, 1936–39; and Corregidor, 1940–42.)

EARLY WAR PLANS

Because of a continuing perception after the end of World War I that war with Japan would come sooner or later, the first efforts by the Navy to establish a COMINT collection capability in the Pacific were directed at the U.S. Asiatic Fleet. It was far from enough, however, and fell short of OP-20-G's goal of an even greater radio intelligence capability against the Japanese Navy. U.S. planning for this eventuality is treated later.

In 1930, OP-20-G planners selected the 13th Naval District, which included Oregon, Washington, and Alaska, as well as Idaho, Montana, and Wyoming, as a prospective location for two new intercept sites: one, a large site to cover Japanese point-to-point traffic with Europe and China on low and high frequencies during wartime; the other, a small site in Alaska ("but not in the islands") to cover Japanese ship-to-shore communications in both peace and war.[12] Because of budgetary restrictions, Admiral Pratt, CNO, was forced to wait until May 1932 before directing Rear Admiral E. H. Campbell, Commandant 13th Naval District, to establish the first of these sites at Astoria,

6

Oregon, where the Navy had a DF station providing navigation assistance to commercial vessels.[13] Rather than build and equip a new site, OP-20-G planners were by then reduced to postponing delivery of the new equipment and asking Admiral Campbell to accept a plan in which a COMINT mission against Japanese targets was to be conducted using idle communications equipment.[14] The initial COMINT mission was to copy Japanese diplomatic traffic on a commercial RCA circuit between Salinas, California, and Tokyo using idle DF receivers which had been tuned to the commercial band.[15]

In the 14th Naval District, Hawaii, an unofficial site established at Wailupe in 1925 was given official status in 1931 and authorized one billet by Admiral Pratt, CNO.[16] Ineffective because of poor signal hearability, the Wailupe site was moved to Heeia in 1934. After the Japanese attack on Pearl Harbor in December 1941, to further improve reception and communications, the site was moved to Wahiawa.

With the exception of closing the sites in Peking in 1935 and Shanghai in 1940, the geographic posture of Navy COMINT in the Pacific retained this modest form until 1941. Small as the collection effort was, however, it is clear that Naval Communications had succeeded by 1941 in establishing a radio intelligence organization targeting primarily the Japanese Navy in the naval districts in the Pacific basin and the Asiatic Fleet. As noted by Wenger in 1937:

> It was not an integrated organization, however, but a number of technically dependent but operationally independent units under the technical control of OP-20-G but under the military command of the two four-star fleet commanders (Pacific and Asiatic). Management control, such as it was, was exercised by CNO and administrative control by many subdivisions of the Navy department and local commander activities (e.g., Bureau of Navigation, Bureau of Engineering, District Communication and Radio Material Officers, Fleet Intelligence Officers and Station Commanders to name but a few). When you consider that "control" was exercised over vast distances using mail sent by train and ship by personnel who frequently had no appreciation for the special problems faced by those being controlled, the wonder is that the system worked at all.[17]

From the early 1920s, OP-20-G participated in U.S. fleet exercises by furnishing cryptographic systems for contending fleet elements, the Battle (or Black) Fleet and the Scouting (or Blue) Fleet, and by training individual line officers in cryptanalytic skills. During the exercises volunteer cryptanalysts often succeeded in penetrating and exploiting the opposing fleet's cryptographic and communications systems. The most successful volunteers were officers usually chosen for the assignment by Safford. These officers demonstrated a flair for cryptanalysis by solving puzzles Safford placed in the monthly *Communications Bulletins* beginning in July 1924. Safford recruited Joseph W. Rochefort, Thomas Dyer, Joseph Wenger, E. S. L. Goodwin, Wesley A. (Ham) Wright, and Jack S. Holtwick in this way.

Captain Jack S. Holtwick

The U.S. fleet problems of 1929 and 1930 dramatically, albeit briefly, called command attention to the work of OP-20-G and provided important recognition for the work of cryptanalysts both in developing codes and ciphers for the fleet and in demonstrating decisively the vulnerability of insecure communications. U.S. Fleet Exercise #9 in 1929 was marked by successful exploitation by Navy cryptanalysts Safford, Rochefort, and Dyer of the Black Fleet against both the cryptography and communications of the Blue Fleet. Safford, Rochefort, and Dyer read all of the traffic of the opposing force (enciphered by a cumbersome cylindrical cipher) and made considerable progress in solving the signal cipher as well.[18]

In his summary critique of the exercise on 15 May 1929, Admiral Henry A. Wiley, CINC, U.S. Fleet, ruefully acknowledged that the successes realized by the decrypting units represented a "serious lack of knowledge (of radio security)."[19] As a result, Safford

8

was directed to "make a cipher which could be broken but not allow messages to be read before the problem is over."[20]

In his memoirs Commander John W. McClaren, who was head of OP-20-G at the time, recalled the chaos created the next year when the fleet was required to use unfamiliar wartime cryptographic procedures, codes, and ciphers during Exercise #10.[21] Not only was the fleet's lack of readiness amply demonstrated by the resulting confusion, but both decrypting units again did quite well against the fleet's codes, ciphers, and communications procedures as well. The Black Fleet decrypting unit consisted of Lieutenant Paul R. Sterling, Lieutenant Clarence V. Lee, Lieutenant Frederick D. Kime, Lieutenant Frank H. Bond, and Ensign William H. Leahy. They were assisted by six yeomen and three messengers. The Blue Fleet unit consisted of Lieutenant Llewellyn J. Johns, Lieutenant Wesley A. (Ham) Wright, Ensign R. Bennett, Ensign Lee W. Parke, three yeomen, and one marine sergeant. The Black unit recovered the Blue Signal Cipher. The Blue unit recovered the Black Signal Cipher, the Black Contact Code, and the Black Callsign System.

Fleet Exercise #11 was also held in 1930, and again each fleet had a decrypting unit. Johns, Brown, Wright, and Parke once again performed for the Blue Fleet assisted by three yeomen and one radioman, all Navy personnel. In the problem the fleets used codes specifically constructed by Safford which theoretically could not be broken during the exercise. In his critique of 7 April 1930, however, commander in chief of the Black Fleet, Admiral Louis M. Nulton, reflected on the successes of each decrypting unit and leveled considerable criticism against designers of the "Recognition Signals," the "Contact and Tactical Report Code," and, to a lesser degree, designers of the callsign system. His critique stated that the signal cipher and the control code were "simple" and "could have been quickly broken down by expert decryptors [sic]." He further reported that the service cipher used to direct movements was unsatisfactory because of the time required to encipher and decipher messages. The recognition signals were too complicated for quick and effective use, though not impossible to memorize or initiate. The callsigns were also too long and too easily associated with the user, according to Nulton.[22] Despite Nulton's criticisms, the exercises reinforced a growing conviction within the fleet that COMINT was a vital tool for commanders, and COMSEC an important prerequisite to success in battle.[23]

JAPANESE FLEET CAPABILITIES AND INTENTIONS

In addition to working U.S. fleet exercises to make fleet communications more secure, cryptologic personnel overseas copied, analyzed, and, with assistance from Washington, exploited radio traffic from four Japanese fleet maneuvers between 1930 and 1935, demonstrating the benefits to strategic planning of communications intelligence derived from foreign military communications. The stations involved comprised Guam, Olongapo, Peking, USS *Goldstar* (AG–12), Los Banitos (Mariveles), and USS *Augusta* (Flagship Asiatic Fleet). Both *Augusta* and *Goldstar* normally were mobile detachments taken from shore stations. At least thirty-three operators were assigned operations-related tasks for the Japanese maneuvers in 1935, which ran from July to September.[24]

Collectively, these stations intercepted the communications of Japanese ships at sea and from participating Japanese shore stations. The Japanese maneuver activity, at its height, typically extended from fleet anchorages in Japan to Saipan in the Marianas and the Palau Islands east of Mindanao. The COMINT reports prepared by personnel at the sites, and later consolidated by personnel in Washington who often had message text which supported the field's conclusions, superbly demonstrated both the tactical and strategic value of COMINT and established, at least in OP-20-G, the conviction that traffic analysis was an equal partner to cryptanalysis. Not only did these reports reflect the Japanese fleet's strategic capability to wage a large-scale successful war against the U.S. Asiatic Fleet, but they also revealed Japan's intentions to invade Manchuria, to defend the western Pacific in case of a U.S. attempt to interfere, and to conduct electronic countermeasures in the event the U.S. attempted to monitor fleet communications. The 1930 Japanese maneuver was seen by U.S. Navy analysts as a rehearsal for an invasion of Manchuria, which actually did occur in the following year. They also revealed plans for the complete mobilization of the Japanese fleet, a comprehensive knowledge on the part of the Japanese of the current U.S. war plan against the Japanese fleet, and the unpleasant fact that the Japanese Navy was superior in strength to the U.S. Asiatic Fleet. Regrettably, the Navy did not see fit to exploit this valuable planning asset by regularly tasking and funding the resources necessary for its continuation.

The 1933 report, for example, revealed details of Japanese plans to defend the western Pacific from a counterattacking U.S. fleet, actual ship movements, Japanese war plans against China, and a myriad of facts and details about air and sea deployment, tactics, communications practices and procedures, order of battle, and individual maneuver objectives.[25] CINCAF, Admiral Frank B. Upham, was particularly impressed by the efforts of the COMINT analysts, whose work was based entirely on traffic analysis, since the Japanese Navy's operational code (the Blue Book) had not been recovered by the time of the exercises. Not only did he visit Station C to personally compliment the men, telling them that one day their work would be of tremendous importance to the nation, but he prepared a unique endorsement for the report. His endorsement, forwarded to Admiral William H. Standley, CNO, on 20 June 1934, contained several significant "COMINT discoveries" based on traffic analysis, including one entitled "Indications of Approaching Hostilities." This prophetic paragraph predicted that "any attack by (Japan) would be made without previous declaration of war or other intentional warning." In keeping with its traffic analysis origins, another finding stated that "preparations would be noticeable in increased radio activity." Admiral Upham also recommended a plan for observing movements of Japanese merchant ships. He believed Japan would try to save as many of these vessels as possible by withdrawing them to Japan prior to any outbreak of war. Ironically, the U.S. Navy did detect such a movement in November 1941.[26] Unfortunately, by the time of Pearl Harbor, Admiral Upham was dead, and his report and recommendations lay forgotten in CNO's files.

Battleship Yamato

The 1933 Japanese maneuvers were also noteworthy for two other features which in themselves speak volumes on the state of development of communications intelligence in the Japanese and American navies. Analysts aboard the *Goldstar* were aware that the Japanese practiced deliberate electronic countermeasures to prevent the CI unit aboard the *Goldstar* from successfully intercepting their naval maneuver traffic.[27] In this regard, it is interesting to note that Operation Problem #IV in 1933 at the Naval War College showed that the United States could not successfully defend U.S. interests in the western Pacific and specifically could not recapture the Philippine Islands or hope to maintain a base in these islands. This action clearly demonstrated Japanese awareness of the value of communications intelligence. On the negative side, however, the final 1933 U.S. naval report on these maneuvers was not completed until 1937! In May 1937 Wenger, in a personal letter to Holtwick at Station C, commented on his final efforts to finish a second report before the end of April. This final report was a labor of both love and curiosity. Wenger had played a major part in recognizing the value of the work done in the field and had collated this work into a final report in 1934. In 1937 he wanted to evaluate the traffic analysis results against Blue Book recoveries not available earlier to see if the messages contained any unique information.[28] Thus, largely because of a lack of manpower, five years elapsed between the event and the Navy's final COMINT report on a significant Japanese fleet exercise which revealed many unique Japanese Navy capabilities.[29]

Another important contribution to the U.S. Navy's efforts to determine the capabilities of the Japanese Navy occurred in 1936 when the cryptanalysts and linguists in Washington translated a message giving the results of the Japanese battleship *Nagato*'s postmodernization trials. This message greatly alarmed U.S. officials because it contained the *Nagato*'s new top speed, which was in excess of twenty-six knots, the same as four new *Kongo*-class battle cruisers and considerably in excess of the twenty-four-knot top speed currently planned for the redesigned U.S. battleships *North Carolina* and *Washington*. By inference the *Nagato*'s speed would be the prospective speed for other battleships being modernized and the minimum speed for new battleships of the *Yamato* class. As a direct result of this message, U.S. naval officials raised the required speed of modernized U.S. battleships to twenty-seven knots and of new vessels to twenty-eight knots.[30]

CRYPTOLOGIC CHALLENGE: NAVY-ARMY COOPERATION

For several years in the early 1930s, the U.S. Navy was the only source of intercepted traffic from Japanese communications. After the Army obtained an intercept capability against diplomatic targets sometime in 1935, a "friendly rivalry" developed as both services attempted to intercept and read as much as possible "to gain credit" for the intelligence.[31] In the late 1930s the Navy discovered that the same Japanese consulate which had twice yielded the Red Book in the early 1920s was also a likely source for "effective and reserve" ciphers and keys for all current diplomatic systems except the two machine systems A and B. Once again, by "borrowing" them the Navy was able to provide

12

the Army and the Asiatic Fleet with Japanese diplomatic ciphers and keys for manual systems before they came into use.

The decade of the 1930s also witnessed a resurgence of U.S. Army interest in cryptanalysis. In 1930, after the collapse of Yardley's New York "Black Chamber,"[32] William F. Friedman was tasked to create an Army cryptologic capability in the office of the Chief Signal Officer. Starting with four civilian students whose names have become bywords in the U.S. cryptologic community – Frank Rowlett, Solomon Kullback, Abraham Sinkov, and John Hurt – Friedman began the slow and difficult training process which would ultimately lead to the compilation of War Department codes and ciphers and the solution of foreign military and diplomatic codes and ciphers.

Seated: A. J. McGrail, W. Preston Corderman, William F. Friedman. Standing: Mark W. Rhoads, Solomon Kullback, John B. Hurt, Edward J. Vogel, Frank B. Rowlett, Abraham Sinkov.

It was to this embryonic work force that the Navy turned in 1931 for help against two cryptographic targets which at the time almost completely occupied OP-20-G's efforts – Japanese diplomatic and naval communications. The introduction of the Blue Book, as the Japanese Navy Operations code was known, in February 1931 (replacing the Red Book) and an unexpected surge in cipher traffic on diplomatic circuits had created an immense work load for Navy cryptanalysts. This forced the Navy to realize that it could no longer handle both targets and to seek a division of effort with the Army, with which it would furnish intercepted traffic until the Army could develop its own collection capabilities.[33]

Not willing to give up all diplomatic communications, however, the Navy proposed that the Army analyze all counterpart Army radio communications and all diplomatic radio communications except for those of the four major naval powers, England, France, Italy, and Japan. This arrangement, the Navy claimed, would help it reduce an estimated two-year time lag in breaking the Japanese Blue Book.[34]

For a number of reasons, negotiations were not immediately fruitful. A primary cause for the lack of progress in the negotiations was that Army intercept sites, when established in the U.S. or even those existing in the Philippines, would not be able to hear low-power military radio transmissions. This unpleasant fact made the Navy's proposition partially irrelevant except in China. There Station A could and did irregularly intercept both Chinese and Japanese ground forces communications, which were provided to Army analysts. Talks continued without resolution until 1933, when a tentative position was developed for presentation to the Joint Army-Navy Board under a much broader heading, "Joint Effectiveness of Army and Navy Communications Systems." The joint proposal encompassed not only COMINT but communications and communications security matters as well. Possibly in return for its promise of cooperation on COMINT target distribution as outlined in 1931, the Army obtained concessions from the Navy in several vital areas including training intercept operators and in preparing a COMSEC Annex to Army War Plans. In addition, the Navy agreed to provide training for enlisted communicators and communications officers.[35]

In 1933 the official aim of both the Navy and the Army in the negotiations could be summed up in two words: "cooperation" and "uniformity." Uniform communications, uniform censorship rules in wartime, uniform authentication systems, and common recognition signals for aircraft, local defense forces, and defense districts were goals which motivated both sides. Since the Navy already had such tools in place within its framework of naval districts and the Army lacked such a structure, it clearly made sense for the Army to consider building on the Navy's experience.

Regarding COMINT matters, however, joint agreements were harder to resolve. The fragile system of cooperation on COMINT targets almost collapsed within days of its tentative approval when it was disclosed by the Army that, inexplicably, the State Department had completely rejected the proposal insofar as it pertained to the Army's collecting diplomatic communications. According to internal Navy correspondence, Army negotiators from the office of the Chief Signal Officer discussed the proposed division of effort with the chief of the Army's War Plans Division, who informed the State

Department. State's rejection of the plan was reported in a memorandum to DNC by OP-20-G on 10 April 1933. Despite State objections, however, some degree of cooperation between the Navy and Army seemed assured.[36]

BUREAUCRACY PREVAILS

With the Blue Book about to be solved, but undoubtedly aware that much work in defining mutual areas of interest remained to be done, the parties were not about to be deflected from their main military goal by a civilian State Department. A memorandum for the Joint Board was approved by Admiral Pratt on 24 April 1933. Attached to the memorandum was a list of twelve joint studies including the recommendation that "a joint study should be made in regard to radio intercept and radio intelligence problems . . . (because of manpower shortages) division of the work should be agreed upon and . . . exchange of information, in outlying districts particularly, should begin without delay."[37] On 13 July 1933, the Joint Board, with General Douglas MacArthur as senior member present, responded by recommending to the secretary of war that nineteen separate joint committees be established to increase "the joint effectiveness of Army and Navy Communications Systems . . . ." Among the committees which were to report back to the Joint Board for final action were two which pertained directly to radio intelligence: (1) Radio Intercept and Radio Intelligence Problems, chaired jointly by Major Spencer B. Akin, Signal Corps, and Commander Howard F. Kingman and (2) Communication and Radio Intelligence Development Board, chaired jointly by Major Akin and Commander F. D. Pryor (Commander Kingman was a member). The following day, 14 July 1933, the secretary of war, George H. Dern, and secretary of the navy, Claude A. Swanson, approved the Joint Board's recommendation.[38] Unfortunately, with their cryptanalytic work load once again in hand and despite the existence of the committees, Navy officials were unable to arrive at a satisfactory consensus with the Army on COMINT cooperation, and the subject appears to have languished until circumstances in 1940 once again demanded attention.

Major General Spencer B. Akin,
U.S. Army Signal Corps

STATUS QUO IN THE PACIFIC

Until the end of 1938 the Japanese maintained a cryptographic status quo which enabled U.S. Navy cryptanalysts to live in the best of worlds. After the Blue Book system was reconstructed by OP-20-G, it was a relatively simple matter for the better part of five years to follow the activities of the Japanese Navy. As one observer noted during the 1930s in the Philippines, "Japanese traffic was everywhere you looked." There were so many options available that a selection process was required to control collection.[39] In Washington, Op-20-G's interest in Japanese diplomatic traffic until 1938–39 remained almost a purely technical one – that is, solving ciphers and recovering keys simply for their cryptographic value. The one exception was the support provided overseas cryptanalysts, particularly at Station C, who were supplied Japanese cipher and key recoveries for their value in developing COMINT in support of the Asiatic Fleet. Station C's responsibilities included keeping CINCAF informed of developments in diplomatic as well as naval messages copied by Peking, Guam, and the Philippines.[40]

A NEW ATTEMPT AT COOPERATION

Major General Joseph Mauborgne

During 1938–39, U.S. successes against both the naval and diplomatic targets began to unravel as the Japanese changed their long-standing cryptographic systems. These developments brought the two U.S. military departments back to the bargaining table in mid-1940. As usual, both sides agreed to go their own way on international commercial and counterpart communications. Regarding diplomatic communications, General Joseph O. Mauborgne, Chief Signal Officer, U.S. Army, proposed an elaborate study to determine which targets could be heard by the individual stations of each service. According to Mauborgne's proposal, responsibility would be assigned according to hearability, frequency, time of day, type of transmission, and, in the case of duplication, preponderance of copy without egard for the underlying value of any ntelligence to the intercepting agency.

16

Convinced that the OP-20-G work load was already excessive, Safford originated several appeals to Rear Admiral Leigh Noyes, DNC, between July and September concerning the pitfalls of this approach. In October 1940, for example, he advised Noyes that the Navy did not want to do German, Mexican, and Italian traffic. He also said that the Signal Corps had little to do if it did not copy high-powered diplomatic transmitters since its stations could not hear the relatively low-powered military radios. He advised Noyes that the Navy should relinquish the entire diplomatic target rather than agree to the proposed Mauborgne scheme.

Before the study could be undertaken, the Army General Staff ordered the Signal Corps to copy the diplomatic circuits of Japan, Germany, Italy and Mexico.[41] Although it meant wholesale duplication of collection, this directive left little room for the two departments to negotiate (no doubt to Safford's immense relief) and led eventually to the recommendation of August 1940 in which the U.S. Navy became responsible for deciphering and translating Japanese diplomatic and consular service messages on odd days of the month and the Army on even days (see Chart A). This narrow and highly simplified arrangement at least relieved Safford of the specter of two conflicting translations of the same message being delivered to the president. It did not, however, as will be seen, relieve the Navy's cryptanalytic and linguistic workload, particularly in 1941 as the crisis between Japan and the United States deepened and the number of diplomatic messages to and from Japan increased. The recommendation was nevertheless approved on 3 October 1940.[42]

Chart A

Army and Navy Sites Authorized to Intercept Diplomatic
Traffic, August 1940

ARMY			NAVY		
Site Location	Site Designator	Number of Collectors	Site Location	Site Designator	Number of Collectors
Fort Monmouth, NJ	1	19	Winter Harbor, ME	W	8
Presidio, CA	2	9	Amagansett, NY	G	4
Fort Sam Houston, TX	3	14	Cheltenham, MD	M	20
Corozal, CZ	4	20	Jupiter, FL	J	4
Fort Shafter, HI	5	19	Bainbridge Island, WA	S	12
Fort Hunt, VA	7	24	Heeia, HI	H	8
Totals	6	105		6	56

Despite a prevailing shortage of cryptanalytic manpower between 1924 and 1941, the U.S. Navy's efforts against Japanese naval codes and ciphers were marked by some brilliant successes. Much was due to the inspired work of people assigned to OP-20-G, such as Safford, Agnes Driscoll (neé Meyer), Dyer, Wright, and Holtwick. Some of the success, however, must be attributed to the ONI, which three times in this period "borrowed" Japanese naval and diplomatic manual codes and ciphers from the Japanese consulate in New York. The Army too deserves credit and praise for its work against high-level machine systems used in enciphering Japanese diplomatic messages.

From 1924 to 1940, U.S. cryptanalysts adopted a system of color designations for certain high-level Japanese cryptographic systems. The Japanese diplomatic machine ciphers were designated Red for the A machine and, in 1939, Purple for the B machine which replaced it at many embassies. In 1939, a naval attaché machine cipher was introduced. It was designated Coral by the U.S. and was in use until 1945.[43] The Japanese Navy's main operational code was designated Red until 1930, Blue until 1938, and Black until 1940, when its designation was changed to JN-25, the Fleet General Purpose System.[44]

The Japanese Navy also employed several other cryptsystems to conduct its business which were not swept into the U.S. system of color designations. At OP-20-G, for example, one worker decrypted all messages in the Japanese navy-merchant vessel liaison code.[45] U.S. cryptanalysts read the code in its entirety from the fall of 1939 to the tenth of August 1941.[46] Six other Japanese naval systems were intercepted regularly. Two of these – an auxiliary ship cipher and a minor general-purpose system – were not worked. A third, an intelligence code, was considered of little importance after its contents were discovered, and it was ignored. The three remaining systems were worked intensively. They were the Japanese naval administrative system, a materiel system, and the fleet general-purpose system. The administrative and materiel systems had similar encipherment forms, and both encipherments were broken from time to time. When this occurred, two workers were assigned to recovery of the underlying codes. Success in the administrative system led to a limited capability to solve the general-purpose code. The materiel code was worked during the spring of 1940 in an unsuccessful attempt to learn details about the performance characteristics of the battleships *Yamato* and the *Musashi*, superbattleships built in violation of existing treaties, which were launched in 1941 and 1942, respectively. Regrettably, all recoveries on Japanese naval systems before Pearl Harbor yielded cryptanalytic technical information rather than current intelligence.[47]

In the grips of a rapidly expanding work load, the limited number of skilled U.S. cryptanalysts and linguists made it impossible to produce current intelligence except in the diplomatic field.[48] The explosive growth of Japanese diplomatic and naval cipher traffic (1200 percent growth between 1930 and 1935)[49] continued in both volume and numbers of systems throughout the 1930s. By the end of 1942, the Japanese Navy employed fourteen different minor systems which generated over 40,000 messages per year in addition to messages obtained from the general-purpose system which, by November 1941, had reached 7,000 messages per month.[50]

RECOVERING THE "BLUE BOOK"

At the end of October 1938, however, without warning the Japanese Navy changed its operational code. Why the Japanese chose this moment to make the change is unknown. Perhaps they feared their old system had been penetrated, or perhaps this was the beginning of a cycle of changes. The change replaced the Blue Book, which had been used since 1931, with the Black Code.

The outgoing Blue Code was never used without a cipher to be stripped off before the code could be reconstructed. Navy cryptanalysts Safford, Dyer, and Driscoll solved the Blue Code in 1933, making possible the important successes against the Imperial Fleet exercises in 1934 and 1935. Their success had followed what was possibly the most difficult cryptanalytic task ever undertaken by the United States up to that time. In Safford's opinion, Driscoll's work in solving the system may have been even more brilliant than the Army's subsequent solution of the Purple machine because "there were no cribs or translations to help out."[51] The introduction of IBM "tabulating machines" against the Blue Book was also a major advancement at the time.

INTRODUCING JN-25

Two additional codes augmented the Japanese Black Code beginning on 1 June 1939: the "Flag Officers Code," which saw very limited use and was never broken, and a five-digit enciphered general-purpose code given the designator "JN-25." The Flag Officer's Code was one of Hawaii's principal tasks until mid-December 1941.

The JN-25 system required three books to operate: a code book, a book of random numbers called an additive book, and an instruction book. The original code book contained some 30,000 five-digit numbers which represented Kana particles, numbers, place-names, and myriad other meanings. A key characteristic of this system was that, when the digits in a group were added together, the total was always divisible by three. The book of random numbers consisted of 300 pages, each of which contained 100 numbers on a 10 x 10 matrix. These numbers were used as additives – they were added to the code groups digit by digit without the carryover used in customary addition – thus enciphering the code. The instruction book contained the rules for using the aperiodic cipher. The number of each page and the number of the line on the page where the selection of additives began served as "keys" which were included in each message at the beginning and end. This code subsequently became the most widely distributed and extensively used of all of Japan's naval cryptosystems.[52]

19

Using improved IBM card sorting equipment and newly developed analytic techniques and noting similarities to an earlier four-digit "S" system stolen from a consulate, Driscoll and her colleagues were soon stripping off daily keys and additives in the Able, or first cipher, and slowly reconstructing the code.[53] After investing a year in attempting to understand its components, OP-20-G put aside all work against the current JN-25 cipher during the summer and fall of 1940 in favor of slow but steady progress toward actual reading of the underlying code. After keys were recovered on each new cipher, the traffic itself was filed for later study.

Though they were working on year-old traffic, the cryptanalysts recovered a segment of the Able code which led to discovery of pattern messages, such as medical reports, and stereotyped messages containing noon positions for convoys. On 1 October 1940, the Japanese introduced the fifth Able cipher (Able Five). It was quickly diagnosed by OP-20-G analysts. Once the new keying system was understood, Washington policymakers decided that all units, including Hawaii, should begin working on the current cipher in the hope that by January 1941 the first JN-25 message of the new year would be read on the same day it was sent. By December 1940, U.S. cryptanalysts had recovered the system of text additives, two systems of keys, and the actual code groups for the numbers 000 through 999. At this point the only factor which seemed to prevent complete exploitation of JN-25 was lack of manpower. Out of the total cryptanalyst population in Washington at this time (thirty-six in December 1940), only from two to five people could be spared to work on this still unreadable system.[54]

TURNING VICTORY INTO DEFEAT

On 1 December 1940, probably before Washington's work could be distributed to the field stations, Japan canceled the Able code which had been used since 1 June 1939. This action completely frustrated any hope of code exploitation by 1 January 1941. The new code was named JN-25 "Baker." It proved to have several unfamiliar features in key generation as well as new and larger code and additive books. For the next two months, however, until 31 January 1941, many messages were intercepted in which the Japanese employed Able code additives already recovered in Able Five. OP-20-G lost no time in exploiting this cryptographic blunder by placing the entire Corregidor effort and most of the Washington effort on the current cipher and code recoveries.[55]

With the progress made on recovery of the new code values, U.S. officials believed that the combined efforts of all units would again bring the system close to the point of reading current traffic by early summer 1941. Code recovery continued to progress well. Throughout the summer and fall of 1941, new discoveries about the nature of the code were routinely committed to a Registered Intelligence Publication (RIP) and given wide if slow-moving distribution to the field units.

The actual reading of current Japanese messages before Pearl Harbor, however, was not to be. U.S. cryptanalysis of the ciphers had outstripped the U.S. capability for code recoveries. That is, OP-20-G and Corregidor (as well as London and Singapore) had not recovered enough of the basic code, and JN-25 decrypts could not be produced in time to play a part in U.S. and policy or military decisions during this crucial period. Thousands of intercepted Japanese Navy messages in JN-25 were not exploited because, as a result of manpower shortages and higher priorities, the underlying code values remained unrecovered.[57]

These proved to be costly factors indeed, because analysts at Hawaii, Corregidor, and Washington never discovered the vital information contained in the untranslated messages. We now know that they contained important details concerning the existence, organization, objective, and even the whereabouts of the Pearl Harbor Strike Force, the Japanese Navy's First Air Fleet. Hidden in these messages was the full magnitude of the enterprise planned by the Japanese to begin on 7–8 December 1941. Had these messages been read on a current basis, it is possible – even probable, given the analytic skills so evident in these centers – that the early course of the war would have been significantly altered. Unfortunately, most of the U.S. Navy's cryptanalytic effort was devoted to another Japanese cryptographic problem: recovering the daily cipher, translating the texts, and reading the Japanese diplomatic messages.

INTRODUCING "PURPLE"

In February 1939, only a few months after discovering the JN-25 and Black Code on naval communications, another shock struck the U.S. cryptanalytic community when the Japanese introduced the Type B machine on their high-level diplomatic circuits. Known as the "Purple" machine, it was eighteen months before the efforts of William Friedman's staff at the U.S. Army's Signal Intelligence Service (SIS) and the Navy Yard Machine Shop succeeded in producing full translations of intercepted diplomatic messages and the first prototype deciphering machine.

The prolonged delay resulted primarily from the complexity of the new Japanese machine. Its impending introduction had been anticipated for several months in 1938, when distribution of the equipment was noted in intercepted messages. Only the more important Japanese embassies received the new machine, including Rome, London, Washington, and Berlin. Those which did not receive the Purple equipment continued to use the Type A machine. In fact, when maintenance was required on the new equipment, a Japanese embassy frequently reverted to the Type A machine.[58]

Recovering from their initial confusion, U.S. cryptanalysts quickly began to exploit the new machine despite its complexities. By 10 April 1939, Frank B. Rowlett and Robert O. Ferner had produced partial texts based on similarities between the A and B systems.[59] However, on 1 May 1939, apparently recognizing the vulnerability of their new system, the Japanese introduced significant complications to the recovery process. By 27 November 1940, however, U.S. Army analysts produced two translations which represented the first solutions to the B Machine.[60] OP-20-G played a minor but important role during this period. Purple analog machines, based on wiring designs developed by the Army, were made at the Navy Yard in Washington, D.C., and distributed to the War and Navy Departments, i.e., to SIS and to OP-20-G, and by mid-1941, to Admiral Thomas C. Hart, CINCAF. The British in London were given equipment originally intended for Hawaii. After the Army solved the system, Navy and Army cooperated in recovering the daily changing keys. Messages from both the Purple and Red machines were known as MAGIC.[61] Once the Purple machine became readable and the need for translated current Japanese diplomatic messages became urgent, the War Department requested additional Navy assistance in the form of cryptanalysts and linguists.

DISARMAMENT: PAYING THE PRICE

The events of 1938 and 1939, which virtually devastated – if only temporarily – the U.S. cryptanalytic efforts against Japan, were only the latest in a series of setbacks and disappointments which had begun with the decade. As the war in Europe expanded and Japanese behavior toward China, the United States, England, and France grew more intransigent, a realization developed in Navy circles that budgetary decisions since the end of World War I, and particularly since 1929, had almost crippled the U.S. fleet. The most severe suffering was felt in manpower-intensive activities such as the COMINT effort. While Germany and Japan openly rebuilt their military establishments during the depression years, the U.S. Congress, preoccupied with disarmament and rebuilding the nation's economy, consistently imposed harsh fiscal constraints on the Navy. In the name of disarmament, Congress called for reductions in both capital expenditures and manpower. For OP-20-G the manpower restrictions had such a severe impact that Safford was to feel their effects up until the eve of the Japanese attack.[62] Moreover, the lack of money for investment meant that not only the operational structure but the support framework also would suffer. For example, a secure electrical communications network could not be built. This meant a continuation of those interminable delays in the exchange of cryptanalytic data and intercepted traffic because surface shipments from and to China and the Philippines (and Hawaii) customarily took weeks and even months. Finally, as if these problems were not enough, Congress, in 1934, passed the Communications Act, which declared communications intelligence an illegal activity.[63]

CONFUSING DIPLOMACY

The same sort of frustrating inconsistencies appeared in U.S. foreign policy toward China and Japan with far more serious consequences, particularly in their impact on Navy planning. Until 1939, the U.S. government followed a pattern of conflicting policies regarding the two nations. Committed on the one hand to an Open Door Policy toward China, the U.S. conversely recognized in 1908 and again in 1917 that Japan had special rights and interests in eastern Asia because of its "territorial propinquity." The Lansing-

22

Ishii Agreement of 1917, in fact, specifically recognized Japan's special position in Manchuria and on the Shantung Peninsula. Moreover, until 1941 the U.S. consistently supplied Japan with the war materials necessary to undertake and sustain operations not only against China but against the Netherlands and France as well. At the same time, the United States maintained a naval rivalry with Japan which, because of various factors, had already begun to tilt in Japan's favor following the end of World War I.

To the U.S. Navy these policies contained serious strategic implications. In the early 1920s the United States was faced with the unpleasant prospect not only of the continuation of a prewar Anglo-Japanese alliance with unfavorable balance of power implications, but with the equally distressing prospect of a superior Japanese fleet in the Pacific, occupying the German islands which lay astride U.S. lines of communication to Australia and making defense of the Philippines virtually impossible. Aided by Canada and Australia at the Washington Conference in late 1921, the U.S. succeeded in replacing the Anglo-Japanese alliance with a four-power treaty with Britain, France, and Japan. This treaty unfortunately limited U.S. and U.K. base building in the Pacific in return for reluctant Japanese acceptance of apparently unfavorable ratios in naval strength. Although not at first seen as an advantageous treaty for Japan, several factors conspired to make it so. Among these were an obsolescent British dreadnaught fleet which effectively eliminated the British Asiatic Fleet as a force; a moratorium on battleship construction which saw the United States scrap twenty-eight vessels including eleven capital ships in various stages of completion;[64] a U.S. commitment to a two-ocean navy which meant that not all new ships joined the Pacific Fleet; and the base-building restrictions of the four-power treaty. Collectively these measures left Japan in a position of local superiority and in a dominant position regarding the coast and approaches to China, the treaty notwithstanding.[65]

Forced by domestic economic considerations to cut back on military spending, the U.S. continued to adhere to arms limitations agreements and self-imposed building moratoriums well into the 1930s while the Axis powers skillfully circumvented them by modernization programs and new construction. By 1939 both the U.S. and British navies had fallen behind the Japanese Navy, not just in numbers of modern vessels but particularly in the technology of naval architecture and naval armaments, ship design, hull speeds, torpedoes, and the caliber of ships' guns. One bright spot during this period, as noted earlier, was that the U.S. was quick to react to the COMINT-derived information concerning battleship speed revealed in late 1936. Regrettably, there was no corresponding move to upgrade the Navy's COMINT program.

STRUGGLING FOR RESOURCES

Throughout this period, while struggling to establish a presence in the Navy, OP-20-G had failed to find a method of assuring a steady supply of manpower. Until the 1930s, when students began to graduate from the intercept operators' school in Washington, OP-20-G drew its enlisted manpower from two career fields – communications specialists and yeomen. Accordingly, since these students were not given career field designators appropriate to their unique role in naval communications (i.e., intercept operators), it was not unusual for almost twenty years to see correspondence from OP-20-G to naval district commanders rescuing these people from being assigned duties in their ostensible fields.

Until late 1941, the number of intercept operators in the Pacific was never very high, thus making their daily availability a matter of some concern to the resident officer-in-charge (OIC). In the Philippines in 1933, for example, it reached an unusually large total of eighteen men whose orders of assignment to the 16th Naval District carried the caveat "only for intercept or RI [radio intelligence] research work." Ordinarily, from 1930 to 1936, when the first DF site opened at Sangley Point on Luzon, the average assigned strength was only nine. Lack of numbers, however, did not reduce either the amount or nature of the work required. In 1937, a fifteen-man work force at Station C was divided into four three-man watches. "Other duties" for this group included electronic and typewriter maintenance, translation, and traffic indexing.[66]

The number of officers involved in radio intelligence in the Philippines was even smaller. For the eight years between 1934 and 1941, it was typically limited to two Washington-trained cryptanalysts. To extend their presence in the fleet for as long as possible, they would usually serve two tours: the first as OIC of Station C, followed by the job of radio intelligence officer on the staff of the Asiatic Fleet. In the staff assignment the RI officer worked with an ONI officer trained in the Japanese language who was usually senior in grade, a situation which, under certain operational circumstances, could prove awkward. To forestall any rank-generated problems, an agreement was struck in the Asiatic Fleet which placed final COMINT responsibility on the OIC of Station C.[67]

Name	OIC Station C	CINCAF RI Officer
Lieutenant Thomas B. Birtly	–	July 31 – Oct 31
Lieutenant Bern Anderson		Apr 32 – Oct 32
Lieutenant Joseph N. Wenger		Oct 32 – Jun 34
Lieutenant JG Thomas A. Huckins		Aug 34 – Nov 35
Lieutenant JG E. S. L. Goodwin	Jun 34 – Nov 35	Nov 35 – Mar 37
Lieutenant JG Roy S. Lamb	Nov 35 – unk	unk – Dec 37
Lieutenant Jack S. Holtwick	unk – Nov 37	Dec 37 – Mar 39
Lieutenant J. A. Williams	Nov 37 – Feb 39	Mar 39 – Jan 40
Lieutenant Jefferson R. Dennis	Feb 39 – Jan 40	Jan 40 – unk
Lieutenant Bernard F. Roeder	Jan 40 – unk	unk – Oct 41
Lieutenant Rudolph J. Fabian	unk – Feb 42	
Lieutenant J. M. Leitwiler	Feb 42 – Apr 42	

The method of selecting an officer as a trainee in cryptanalysis was slightly different though colored with the same sort of influences and priorities found among enlisted men. Between 1920 and 1940, a career as a naval line officer (e.g., gunnery officer) in the fleet was the prime pathway to success for Academy graduates. Naturally, the fleet had first priority on any and every line officer. Normally, an Academy graduate spent his first seven years at sea, two years ashore, then three years at sea.[68] Tours in gun turrets on battleships and cruisers usually led to more responsible positions on board ship (such as navigator) and eventually a command, particularly after a two-year shore assignment at the postgraduate school in Annapolis. On the other hand, tours in intelligence or in radio intelligence, often given to people who had failed to obtain the assignment of choice, were viewed as dead-end assignments leading to poor efficiency reports upon reassignment to the fleet.[69] This situation had a noticeably chilling effect on career decisions for officers and by 1936 had come to the attention of Admiral William H. Standley, CNO. Standley, one of the few senior officers of his time aware of the importance of radio intelligence, advised his personnel chief that some action must be taken to eliminate the stigma of such assignments.[70] Nevertheless, it is clear that, with few exceptions, both officers and enlisted men preferred almost any other assignment when faced with the prospect of an assignment in radio intelligence.[71] Although communications officers did enter the COMINT field, and some, such as Wenger and John R. Redman, did eventually become admirals, most of the officers who led the Navy's COMINT effort in 1941 were either reservists or line officers who had willingly or unwillingly given up their chance for flag rank to serve in the obscurity of radio intelligence assignments.[72] Moreover, until Safford's appointment as head of OP-20-G in 1936, the Code and Signal Section had not had a permanent, full-time chief though there is little doubt that Safford retained control while on detached sea duty. In an attempt to fill the officer-cryptanalyst quotas spelled out in war plans at theater level, the Navy conducted an elementary cryptanalysis training program for reservists in several naval districts between 1934 and 1939. The numbers over the five-year period, however, amounted to less than 119 throughout the entire Navy.[73]

PLANNING FOR WAR

Another aspect of the perennial manpower problem concerned the capability of OP-20-G to perform in wartime, particularly during a war with Japan. While it has proven virtually impossible to trace, the following discussion of strategic planning strongly suggests that the impact of a new naval strategy in 1940–41 on COMINT resources in the Pacific was pervasive, overpowering, and largely negative. The Japanese scenario had existed since the turn of the century when the United States, after its war with Spain, found itself in possession of many islands in the Pacific Ocean, most notably the Philippines and Guam, which it could neither administer nor adequately defend. The military aspects of the situation called for close cooperation between the Army and Navy and in 1903 led to creation of the Joint Army-Navy Board, usually known as the Joint

Board. From its inception the board concerned itself with prospects of war with Japan, particularly after Japan emerged victorious from the Russo-Japanese war in 1904–05. A fundamental assumption by the board was that the Philippines would always be Japan's first wartime objective.

Adopting a series of colors to identify its plans, the board developed the first Japanese war plans (Orange) in 1904–05. The usual pattern was for the joint plan to be augmented by individual service plans which were constantly reviewed and refined each year depending on military necessity, the moods of Congress, and the international situation. As the plans grew in complexity, the service plans themselves were augmented by individual service plans such as Naval Communications and Naval Intelligence.

The version of the Navy's Orange War Plan which was current in 1941 actually had its inception in May 1929 as WPL13. Changed eight times in ten years, Orange number six in May 1937 brought the Navy's plan into line with the Joint Army-Navy Basic War Plan Orange. From the point of view of OP-20-G, this change was unique since, for the first time in section 7, chapter II, part I (The Strategic Plan), ONI was tasked to plan for the "collection, evaluation, and dissemination of all information of military and economic value." This language appears to have inspired extensive revisions to the Communications Service plan, Appendix 4 of which pertained to COMINT.

Addressing issues such as wartime organization and subordination of communications intelligence within the naval establishment, the responsibility for dissemination of COMINT, the subordination of translators attached to COMINT activities, and U.S.-U.K. relationships, the DNC plan now provided for COMINT as an integrated service under the Chief of Naval Operations. The provisions of Appendix 4 also provided for dissemination of COMINT by the Naval Intelligence Service and, not surprisingly, stated that the COMINT organization "worked for the DNI under the DNC."[74] Organizationally, the 1937 plan more than reinforced the decentralized wartime operation visualized originally by DNC planners. Appendix 4 was revised again in 1939, and the COMINT function was somewhat streamlined by the proposal to drop the COMSEC function of OP-20-G into another appendix. Accordingly, a revised Appendix 3 for COMSEC was completed in 1939, although it would be 1942 before OP-20-G was actually relieved of COMSEC responsibilities.

After the war plan review of 1937, OP-20-G commissioned a study of its current posture.[75] This study was probably intended to measure the current COMINT organization against the needs of the war plan. The results reflected a work force quite inadequate to the tasks as outlined in the war plan. Instead of a required seven "intercept nets," only five were found to exist and a total of only eighty-seven radiomen served the intercept and direction finding function of these nets.[76] To be faced with a totally inadequate collection structure was one thing, but OP-20-G found it necessary immediately to enhance its commitment to a research effort. Characterizing it as the "nucleus" of a wartime organization, OP-20-G proposed to enlarge its current research manpower (i.e., purely cryptanalyst) authorizations worldwide to a total of forty-three.[77]

The resource review acknowledged that the foremost operational problems facing OP-20-G were manpower shortages, an expanding and increasingly complex Japanese cryptographic environment, and the resulting cryptanalytic backlogs which continued to engulf the small work force. All of these problems focused on research manpower. Having recognized the susceptibility of Japanese cryptography to machine exploitation, an immediate solution was to recommend the installation of IBM tabulating equipment in all research units as rapidly as funds would permit. The idea was that this equipment would enable fewer people to do more work. By equipping these units with the latest IBM equipment in peacetime and developing other machines to meet improvements in Japanese cryptography, OP-20-G believed that necessary cryptanalytic techniques could be developed and the people properly trained before hostilities began. Theoretically, no delays would occur after war began in exploiting the Japanese cryptographic systems, at least not through lack of equipment.

It is both interesting and instructive to follow the vicissitudes of War Plan Orange (WPL13) from 1937 to 1941 because of the bearing they may have had on the resource decisions made concurrently in DNC and OP-20-G and because they will provide a revealing insight into the events at Pearl Harbor on 7 December 1941.

A familiar and fundamental feature of WPL13 in 1937 was a U.S. Navy offensive into the western Pacific from Pearl Harbor. The initial objective of this operation was to either relieve its defenders or recapture Manila Bay. Although the Army thought the offensive aspects of this Orange plan in 1937 were "an act of madness," they could not argue that Manila Bay was the best and possibly the only base from which to conduct future offensive operations in support of other U.S. interests in the Far East. Here was an obvious area for future compromises.

The Navy Basic War Plan Orange for 1938 contained three new assumptions inspired by extensive Army revisions to the Joint Plan, which eliminated all references to offensive warfare: (1) outbreak of war would be preceded by a period of strained relations; (2) Orange would attack without warning; and (3) a superior U.S. fleet would operate west of Hawaii.

The eighth and final change to WPL13 was made in March 1939. This change reflected the initial shift in U.S. strategic thinking from the Pacific to events in Europe and the Atlantic Ocean, away from offensive operations toward a concept of defensive operations and readiness. At the same time a new planning system replaced the colors adopted over thirty years before with the Rainbow Plans described briefly as follows:

Rainbow 1 (WPL42): Limited action in order to prevent a violation of the Monroe Doctrine as far south as 10 degrees south latitude. This plan was approved by the secretaries of war and navy on 14 August 1939.

Rainbow 2: Rainbow 1 in first priority followed by concerted action by the United States, Great Britain, and France against the Fascist powers. U.S. forces responsible solely for the Pacific.

Rainbow 3 (WPL44): Rainbow 1 in first priority followed by projecting American forces into the western Pacific.

Rainbow 5 (WPL46): Rainbow 1 in first priority followed by U.S. armed forces into east Atlantic or Europe and Africa in concert with Great Britain and France. (Modified to conform to the course of the war in Europe during 1940 until December 1941.)

Planning for WPL13 appears to have continued during 1939 and into early 1940. Attempting to add realism, planners in September 1939 assumed that Japan would dominate the Asian coast and adjacent waters as far south as Indochina. They rejected a hypothesis that Japan already controlled the Netherlands East Indies and was poised to take over Singapore and the Philippines. The planners also considered a third alternative – that Japan had not yet moved southward from Formosa – since the central issue was at what point the United States would intervene. The planners rejected this alternative because they could not decide whether it would necessitate intervention and were not certain that the American people would support such preventive measures as early movement of the U.S. Fleet to the Philippines, to the East Indies, or to Singapore.

At this stage it should be noted that Rainbow 2 for 1939 described solely a naval war in which the United States had made no commitment to China. The plan concentrated on measures necessary to keep pressure on Japanese overseas lines of supply and communication. It did contain for the first time a specific COMINT-related task levied on the Naval Communications Service. The service was to intercept enemy communications and locate enemy units (using DF) and turn over the information to ONI for "dissemination as advisable." Although many concerned voices were raised over the inherent weaknesses of WPL13 and the Pacific war features of Rainbow 2, this is the last recorded activity in Pacific war planning until June 1941.

Rainbow 2 was the final Pacific-first strategic plan. It was never adopted by the Joint Board or published. Beginning in early 1940, the entire focus of American strategy changed following Germany's easy victories in Norway and Denmark. The shift in focus was signaled by a letter from the Joint Planning Committee to the Joint Board on 9 April 1940, recommending that planning begin immediately under Rainbow 5, leaving Rainbows 3 and 4 in skeletal form. With this letter, Pacific-first strategic thought and planning was virtually at an end. The fall of France in June 1940 and the subsequent Battle of Britain raised serious questions about the security of the United States itself, whether or not the British Isles would fall as France had, and the fate of the British Navy. Suddenly, the fate of England and control of the Atlantic Ocean were the most vital planning issues in American policy.

The brief but interesting evolution of Rainbow 5 from being one among equals to the preeminent U.S. war plan is also instructive. It not only involves the final stages of the other four plans, but its details, too, lend insight to the events of December 1941.

After the fall of France in June 1940, General George C. Marshall, Army Chief of Staff, and Admiral Harold R. Stark, Chief of Naval Operations, submitted to President Roosevelt a draft entitled "Bases for Immediate Decisions Concerning National Defense." As amended after the president's views were obtained, it became on 27 June 1940 a plan for national defense. Its six provisions were as follows:

1. Assumption of a defensive posture by the U.S.

2. Provision of support for the British Commonwealth and China.

3. Implementation of Rainbow 4 actions for defense of the hemisphere.

4. Cooperation with certain South American countries.

5. Undertaking of "progressive" mobilization including a draft and other measures to accelerate production of war material and training of personnel.

6. Beginning of preparations for the "almost inevitable conflict" with totalitarian powers.[78]

Although planning for war with Japan was not extinct, the end was now near. On 25 September 1940, a memorandum prepared by Army planners for their boss, Major General George V. Strong, examined U.S. prospects in the event of a British defeat in the Atlantic in the context of the American commitment in the Pacific (i.e., Rainbow 3 vs. Rainbow 4) and concluded that they were incompatible policies. Army planners went one step further and warned against a more active policy of pressure toward Japan. They recommended rapid U.S. rearmament, aid to Great Britain, refraining from antagonizing Japan, remaining on defensive in the Pacific, and finally, moving to ensure the security of the western Atlantic.

In a similar study two months later, Navy war planners under Captain Richmond K. Turner discovered that realistic Pacific operations under Rainbow 3 would be impossible if the naval detachment required under Rainbow 4 were transferred to the Atlantic. With the forces available, they reported, the U.S. Navy could operate in only one theater. This discovery led Admiral Stark to write his famous "Plan Dog" memorandum to Secretary Knox on 12 November 1940. The ideas contained in his memorandum had not changed significantly between June and November although they did reflect some of General Strong's thoughts from September. His conclusion, however, was remarkable: the United States might "do little more in the Pacific than remain on a strict defensive." Clearly, the first U.S. priority was to the British war effort and to prevent the war in Europe from spreading to the Western Hemisphere. Still it is startling to see the Chief of Naval Operations, in the fall of 1940, advocating a policy of avoiding even a limited war with Japan after over thirty years of planning for an unlimited offensive war. The only concession Stark would make was to leave the U.S. fleet at Pearl Harbor because of the U.S. diplomatic commitments in the Far East. His firmness in this purpose was to cost Admiral James O. Richardson, Commander in Chief, U.S. Fleet, his job.[79]

Cause and effect relationships are often difficult to establish, particularly in resource decisions in Naval Communications and OP-20-G. Frequently one must work backwards from the end result. Using this method, it is clear that manpower resources in OP-20-G were adversely affected by the CNO shift in policy and planning from Pacific-first to Germany-first. Chart B graphically displays the fact that in December 1941 over 60 percent of all COMINT manpower had been concentrated in Washington where the only current mission was Japanese diplomatic and Atlantic DF. It is also clear in Chart B that two thirds of the officer cryptanalysts available to OP-20-G were also assigned to Washington, where cryptanalytic research was the primary mission. In earlier discussions of Japanese naval systems, it was noted that the year before only from two to five people could be spared to work on JN-25. There is, moreover, ample reason to believe that emphasis had not changed materially by December 1941. Given the new Germany-first policy, how interested were naval decision makers in OP-20-G, War Plans, and Operations in the Pacific-related intelligence being pumped out by Pearl Harbor, Corregidor, and OP-20-G? These units were individually and collectively flooding the desks and in-baskets of Navy officials in Washington with alarming reports of Japanese war preparations, some of which must have read like cribs from a Rainbow 2 planner's wastebasket. Yet, as became painfully clear throughout 1941, only readable messages were bankable, and only Japanese diplomatic messages were being deposited. On 11 June 1941, Admiral Stark formally canceled WPL13.[79]

Chart B

Distribution of Navy Comint Personnel
December 1941

Category	Atlantic: Navy Dept.	Pacific: Pearl Harbor	Asiatic: Corregidor	In Transit	Total
Officers/	53	12	9	6	80
Cryptoclerks	157	18	19	20	214
Subtotal	210 (47%)	30 (16%)	28 (26%)	26	294 (40%)
Intercept Stations/DF Control	178	72	42	--	292
Outlying DF Stations	60	84	8	--	152
Subtotal	238 (53%)	156 (84%)	50 (64%)	--	444 (60%)
Totals	448 (61%)	186 (25%)	78 (10%)	26 (3%)	738 (100%)

Closely aligned with the planning function are war games. Games are invaluable for testing all elements of a plan. Their scenarios are a mixture of capabilities and objectives which may be deliberately arranged to test a specific plan as a whole or a single element within a plan.

War games were introduced into the U.S. Navy in the late nineteenth century by Lieutenant William McCarty Little, a member of the staff of the Naval War College. As a result, early in the twentieth century, the War College virtually backed into a war planning relationship with the Navy's General Board. The board was to designate a country for which a Naval War Portfolio was to be prepared; ONI would provide the necessary information, and the board would prepare a plan aided by the staff of the War College. In fact, the College did most of the work.

Before World War I, students at the War College raised the issue of planning for wars without guidance from the political establishment. They felt that trying to plan without the answers to such questions as, What are the intentions of the United States in China, Japan, the Monroe Doctrine? was an exercise in futility. Their questions found willing listeners on the board, at ONI, and even in the secretary of the navy. The Navy proposed various remedies to both the legislative and executive branches based on the premise that "plans not based on the interrelation of the enemy's and our own motives are of little value" – but to no avail.

In March 1912, the General Board, under its chairman, Admiral George Dewey, broke with the College over its objections to the vague and narrow terms of a war plan request. In his decision Admiral Dewey dictated that military men should limit their curiosity to "purely military questions. A plan can be prepared for a specific purpose . . . without reference to any matter not bearing directly on the purpose in view. . . . A commander in chief should, therefore, rarely be influenced by ulterior motives."

The effects of this decision were apparent at the War College as recently as the 1960s, when the curriculum was described as "not focusing on the specific political consequences past, present, or future of military actions." In the context of the events of 1940 and 1941 both in the Pacific and in Washington, the effects produced planners whose perceptions of Japanese naval capabilities and national intentions may have been seriously flawed by war planning doctrines which ruled out enemy intentions altogether as unreliable and subject to rapid change. Under these circumstances, COMINT producers who provided strategic warning beginning in September 1941 that Japan was preparing for war should not have been surprised that their warnings were ignored until the eleventh hour.[80]

PACIFIC BUILDUP

After an abortive attempt at across-the-board modernization in the early Depression years, virtually all OP-20-G's attempts to increase manpower and improve equipment during the 1930s were directed toward the Pacific basin where the Japanese threat was seen as paramount. In 1937, OP-20-G opened the long anticipated major research unit in Hawaii with the task of supporting Washington's efforts.[81] Lieutenant Commander Thomas Dyer was detached from fleet duty and assigned to COM-14 as a cryptanalyst. His duties were to establish a decrypting unit and undertake research work on "M1 Orange Naval Cryptographic System."[82] Message files for 1935, 1936 and 1937 were supplied by OP-20-G and sent to Dyer via the USS *Chaumont*. COM-16 sent copies of all traffic, including messages intercepted by Stations A, B, and C to Dyer, and Washington men-

Captain Thomas H. Dyer, USN

tioned that IBM equipment would be forthcoming at once. At the outset, when not occupied by other duties assigned by Com-14, Dyer, who was not a Japanese linguist, singlehandedly attempted to recover all keys as they appeared. He naturally forwarded all solutions to Washington for translation. In 1939, when the M1 system had been exhausted, Dyer was assigned cryptanalytic responsibility for the Japanese Navy's Flag Officers Code. Lieutenant Joseph Richardson appeared the following July as language officer.

IBM equipment promised in 1937 was not immediately forthcoming. In February 1938, however, OP-20-G notified Dyer that he was to receive IBM tabulating machinery and two clerks. Taking a little

of the glow from the moment, Dyer was also told that after becoming familiar with the equipment he was to train the clerks himself. Typically, he was instructed to provide "material assistance to Washington" as soon as possible.[83] Again, the manpower problem imposed severe limitations on potential U.S. successes against the Japanese codes.

NATIONAL EMERGENCY

In September 1939, all restrictions on increasing personnel and installations were removed when the U.S. declared a national emergency. A few weeks later most of the earlier "Neutrality Legislation" was overturned. Nevertheless, manpower shortages continued to plague the Navy COMINT program, particularly in the Pacific, well into

1941.[84] In June 1940, Admiral Claude C. Bloch, COM-14, requested more manpower (twenty-one billets) to expand his COMINT operation.[85] In his favorable endorsement to the Bureau of Navigation, which handled all Navy personnel matters, Admiral Harold R. Stark, CNO, made the following observation: "The main obstacle to expansion [of communications intelligence activities] is not the matter of increased allowances but finding suitable personnel to fill existing allowances. Many of the reserve personnel in DNC's mobilization slate are reluctant to leave their civilian occupations prior to full mobilization, and COM-14 has been unable to find any suitable volunteers."[86] Later in 1940 Safford complained, "We are allowed 75 and actually have 55."[87]

Compounding the continuing manpower shortage by adding inordinate delays to the system of exchanging crypt recoveries between Washington and the field was a severe and perennial communications problem which affected all Navy COMINT initiatives, particularly those against the Japanese. Therefore, even before they broke down completely when war began, the primitive methods of U.S. Navy communications and the centralization of cryptanalytic functions proved to be major liabilities which prevented realization of the ultimate organizational goal, support for the fleet commander. The addition of officer-cryptanalysts to Station C and to the centers in Hawaii was not successful in this regard because code and key system recoveries from Washington, when available, were delayed by the surface transportation system of commercial vessels and railroads. As a result, completely current English texts were probably a rarity in the Philippines before the war and were never seen in Hawaii until March 1942.

The individual radio intelligence officer-analysts assigned to the Asiatic Fleet and the 14th and 16th Naval Districts between 1930 and 1940 were, by today's standards, almost completely isolated from Washington. Communications between Washington and its far-flung resources in the Pacific continued to be primitive until long after 7 December 1941. Messages and intercept logs, reports and professional correspondence, if classified, were painstakingly enciphered by the radio intelligence officer himself using special equipment and instructions.[88] If transmitted as messages on manual morse circuits or landlines, they were delivered to the communications center where they were again enciphered. Material such as traffic logs and routine Japanese messages, however, were always sent home by mail. A package was usually forwarded once a week from Hawaii, Guam, and the Philippines. It would be put aboard a commercial ship or a station-keeping vessel like the USS *Chaumont*, which traveled the Pacific from California to China. After 1935, a small amount of mail could be sent via the Pan American Airways "Clipper" using a small strongbox built into the hull specifically for that purpose. Keys to open the strongbox were held by authorized officers at appropriate points along the route. The code known as RIP 30 was developed specifically for air mail letters.[89] The introduction of air mail service in 1935 reduced travel time from weeks to days, but the need for major improvements in communications before COMINT would become a useful instrument during wartime was clear.[90]

33

CIRCUMSTANCES FAVOR DIPLOMATIC TARGETS

Electrical communications within the continental U.S. were only slightly better than those overseas, and only in rare cases did they serve to speed the flow of information to Washington from abroad. In August 1940, the Navy had five sites with diplomatic targets which were all linked directly (or indirectly through Army circuits) to Washington via radio and landline communications. These sites were Winter Harbor, Maine; Amagansett, New York; Cheltenham, Maryland; Jupiter, Florida; and Bainbridge Island, Washington.[91] Radio communications with Hawaii consisted of single channel morse links between Washington, San Francisco, and Pearl Harbor. Landline communications consisted of the relatively higher capacity government and commercial teletype circuits owned or used by each military department. The Army owned 401 mainly east-west circuits with 1,003 machines. The Navy owned forty-four mainly north-south circuits on the coasts, the first of which was not established until 1941. These circuits served naval activities at Washington, Norfolk, Philadelphia, New York, New London, Boston, and Portsmouth, New Hampshire.[92] In March 1941, a commercial teletype line between Winter Harbor, Amagansett, and Bainbridge Island was inaugurated.[93] Despite the availability of teletype circuits from the West Coast to Washington, D.C., there is no indication that packages containing Japanese intercept from the Pacific which arrived by either air or sea throughout the 1930s were opened until they reached Washington through normal overland channels. In 1939, triple-wrapped packages from Guam containing the daily bundles of messages were received by the "Courier Station" in San Francisco, where they were opened and placed in registered mail. The inner package was marked, "To be opened only by OP-20-G." In the Philippines during the 1930s, intercept material was mailed to Washington in a similar manner.[94]

INFORMATION GAPS

By 1941, the mission constraints in Corregidor and Hawaii improved by their limited cryptanalytic capabilities and the pervasive shortages of all types of manpower in Washington contributed to a growing sense of alarm in OP-20-G. As the year progressed, certain daily summaries produced by Hawaii and Corregidor, particularly those which sounded warning signals, were no doubt marked for electrical forwarding. But the capacity of manual morse circuits and the inherently slow moving manual decryption features of Navy communications between the mainland and overseas stations were contributing to a serious information gap between Washington and the fleet-supporting field activities.

In July 1941, the nucleus of what would become OP-20-GC (communications) in early 1942 was formed using personnel from OP-20-GY (cryptanalysis). The objective of this new element was to encrypt, decrypt, route, deliver and file COMINT dispatches between OP-20-G and the outside world. In theory this organization was intended to be much faster and much more secure than the Navy Code Room. The whole affair, unfortunately, was undertaken on an incredibly small scale. By December 1941, it consisted of two reserve ensigns, neither of whom were trained or experienced in communications. Under these circumstances – which seem doomed to fail – it is little wonder that OP-20-G's customers were attracted to readable diplomatic messages collected by mainland sites (see Chart A). It is also little wonder that, at this time, the principal source of crisis-related communications intelligence available in Washington prior to Pearl Harbor was Japanese diplomatic traffic.[95]

Three events involving the sites at Cavite and Heeia, Hawaii, from 1938 to 1941 will strikingly illustrate how truly primitive were the communications which served the Navy's COMINT function overseas. In September 1938, Lieutenant Jack S. Holtwick, then the CINCAF Radio Intelligence Officer, complained to OP-20-G about the lack of electrical communications between the unit at Cavite and the flagship. He said that "it now takes days to obtain COMINT information needed to prepare a daily status report." In 1940, Hawaii commented on tracking Japanese naval vessels during annual maneuvers stating that "the only helpful direction finding came from the Philippine unit by Clipper mail!"[96] Finally, on 5 January 1940 Admiral Stark, CNO, requested the Bureau of Engineering to connect the site at Heeia to an Army cable which then terminated at Kailua, eight miles away. Stark also requested the engineers to arrange for an intercom between the communications intelligence unit at Pearl Harbor, the Lualualei direction finding site, and Heeia, also by Army cable, using "other than teletype instruments." These arrangements were meant to replace the public party line telephone service. By 7 December 1941, the work had not been done, and with the loss of telephone service in the attack, there were no communications between Heeia and Pearl Harbor (about thirty road miles) except by vehicle![97]

COOPERATION WITH ALLIES

Until August 1941, efforts to recover JN-25B code values were restricted to the British force at the Far East Combined Bureau (FECB), Singapore, and four U.S. officer-linguists at Corregidor, working in close collaboration with the British. In August 1941, OP-20-G, Washington, began to help with JN-25B code recovery but was hampered by lack of linguists familiar with Japanese naval terminology and usage and by the slow communications available at the time. The only current JN-25 messages read by U.S. analysts on Corregidor during this period were few in number and were invariably ship movement reports: arrivals and departures, together with some fragmentary schedules. In view of the full collaboration and exchange with FECB, Singapore, there is no reason to believe that the British exceeded the U.S. accomplishments.

THE MOVE TO HAWAII

On 7 May 1940, the U.S. fleet moved its headquarters from San Pedro, California, to Pearl Harbor. The move was undertaken with great reluctance by Admiral James O. Richardson, Commander in Chief, U.S. Fleet. Richardson and most Navy officials who opposed the move thought a fleet anchored in Pearl Harbor would be unnecessarily exposed to Japanese naval strength. President Roosevelt, however, considered the move as a necessary countermeasure to growing Japanese bellicosity. Throughout 1940 Richardson bitterly voiced his objections to relocating his headquarters to Pearl Harbor because it challenged the soundness of U.S. policy in the Pacific. He claimed that a Pacific naval offensive – the heart of the Navy's War Plan Orange – was sure to fail because the U.S. did not have the capability to support an offensive west of Hawaii. He also noted a factor not considered by the war planners: the U.S. was now vulnerable to attack in the Atlantic and the Caribbean. In January 1941, Roosevelt ordered him relieved. His replacement was Admiral Husband E. Kimmel who, at the same time, was designated Commander in Chief, U.S. Pacific Fleet (CINCPACFLT).

Lieutenant Commander Edwin T. Layton

36

During this period of great internal upheaval in the Pacific Fleet, two relatively insignificant events occurred which actually marked the beginning of a close COMINT relationship between that fleet and OP-20-G. On 7 December 1940, exactly one year to the day before Japan attacked Pearl Harbor, Lieutenant Commander Edwin T. Layton, a Japanese linguist with past experience in OP-20-G, became the Fleet Intelligence Officer, and a few months later, Commander Joseph J. Rochefort, who was the only man in the Navy who was both a cryptanalyst and a Japanese linguist, became OIC of the 14th Naval District's Radio Intelligence research effort. Layton and Rochefort were old friends from sea duty and from language training in Japan. Rochefort was assigned to the fleet when he was transferred to COM-14. Both knew of the OP-20-G operation, having served under Safford in the 1930s. Layton served only briefly, but Rochefort had received extensive training as a cryptanalyst. They quickly established a close working relationship, and the liaison would soon prove immensely beneficial to the U.S. Pacific Fleet.[98]

Both Rochefort and Layton were called upon regularly to brief Kimmel on what COMINT revealed about the Japanese Navy. In one instance Layton's analysis of callsign and address usage, which he had undertaken during 1941 at Rochefort's request, was sent to Washington on the order of Admiral Kimmel.[99] His conclusion that the Japanese had begun a military buildup in the Mandate Islands (Marianas, Carolines, and Marshalls) was a development which had gone unnoticed by COMINT analysts in Washington. Unexpectedly, rather than foster good relationships between Pearl Harbor and Washington, this episode caused considerable ill feeling toward Layton and Rochefort. It may also marked the beginning of an unhealthy intramural OP-20-G rivalry between the Washington and Hawaiian centers over the issues of COMINT reporting responsibilities and Japanese intentions which persisted well into 1942.[100]

SUPPORT TO THE PACIFIC FLEET

From July 1941 onward, the COMINT research unit in Hawaii under Rochefort prepared daily COMINT summaries for Admiral Kimmel (see Appendix C). They were based on analysis of Heeia collection and to some extent on technical and intelligence information from Corregidor. Hawaii's analytic contributions to the summaries were based on traffic analysis of message externals and direction finding results since the Flag Officer's Code could not be read, and they had no capability against the Japanese Fleet Operational Code (JN-25). These summaries were characterized by Layton after the war as containing "no hard intelligence." This is a harsh judgment. Individually, though it is true that they contained no Japanese message texts, the summaries constituted the substance of Layton's daily reports to CINCPAC. Collectively they revealed a wealth of information concerning Japanese naval activities, particularly those under way in the Mandates, on the islands of Hainan and Taiwan, and along the Chinese coast (see Appendix C).

Lieutenant Joseph Rochefort, OIC Station Hypo

In many respects COM-14's efforts and achievements in 1941 were similar to what had been accomplished at Station C with traffic analysis against the Japanese Imperial Fleet maneuvers in the 1930s. The COM-14 daily summaries clearly showed that Lieutenant Thomas A. Huckins and Lieutenant John A. Williams, who headed the traffic analysis unit, had solved both the strategic and tactical Japanese naval communications structures. They understood the callsign generation system and were able quickly to re-establish order of battle data after routine callsign changes. This insight permitted unit identifications to the squadron level in ground-based-air and destroyer units. It also allowed identifications to the individual ship level in battleships, cruisers, and carriers. The capability to exploit these features of Japanese Navy communications lasted until about three weeks prior to the attack on Pearl Harbor when callup and addressing procedures changed abruptly.[101] Throughout the period they were also able to use their direction finding capability to produce unique information as well as to support evidence from traffic analysis. The traffic analysis unit was able to identify the Japanese Navy mainline shore establishment from Imperial and Combined Fleet Headquarters to principal line and staff subordinates within each of the fleets in both home and deployed locations. Based on the content of their daily summaries, it is conceivable that communications being intercepted by Hawaii (Heeia) in 1941 encompassed the entire Japanese Navy communications system ranging from Japan to South China, to the Mandate Islands, and to the connecting ocean area.[102] Intercepted messages were mailed to Washington for exploitation of their texts.

JAPANESE INTENTIONS REVEALED

As early as July 1941, traffic intelligence reports (i.e., reports founded on traffic analysis) prepared for Admiral Claude C. Bloch, COM-14, and Admiral Kimmel, CINCPACFLT, reflected Japanese air and naval concentrations "awaiting the assumed Southern operations." In fact, from July until 6 December, summaries from Hawaii made frequent allusions to the "formation of Task Forces" and forthcoming "hostile actions" and called attention to similarities between current activities and those which preceded earlier Japanese naval and military campaigns in South China and Indochina.[103] Bearing in mind that Hawaii could not read the message texts, the accuracy of these reports was truly remarkable.

SUPPORT TO ASIATIC FLEET

Corregidor too was very active in following Japanese fleet naval and air movements throughout 1941, producing reports for much of the year in technical channels, which included the CINCAF radio intelligence officer and the Hawaiian Research Center. It was not until October 1941 that Station C's technical reports began to appear as daily intelligence summaries. Rochefort's daily reports often contained information derived from reports from Corregidor.[104] In late November, because of its scope and the station's central location, COM-16's perspective was judged to be superior to Hawaii's and to the fragmentary and often conflicting reports from other sources such as attachés in Shanghai, Chungking, and Tokyo. On 24 November 1941, Admiral Stark, CNO, ordered Admiral Hart, CINCAF, to receive, evaluate, and combine all reports and conclusions, including those from COM-14, reporting directly to CNO with information to Admiral Kimmel, CINCPAC.[105] In the two weeks of peace remaining before Pearl Harbor, this order had little or no effect on events.[106]

JAPANESE STRATEGY

While the United States attempted to maintain a level of strategic equality with Japan in the Pacific by offsetting losses of capital ships sent to the Atlantic with a buildup of long-range air power, the Japanese government formulated plans for war in the Pacific. The Japanese war plan for the Western Pacific campaigns began to unfold well before 10 November 1941 when General Count Hisaichi Terauchi, commanding the Southern Army, and Admiral Isoroku Yamamoto, commanding the Combined Fleet, formally concluded a "Central Agreement" which outlined an ambitious scheme of Japanese conquests.[107] According to the agreement, the first operational stage was divided into three phases: (1) attacks on the Philippines, Malaya, Borneo, Celebes, Timor, Sumatra, and Rabaul (also Guam, Wake, and Makin); (2) capture of Java and the invasion of southern Burma; and (3) conquest of all Burma. The Japanese then envisioned pacification of the area, the creation of a Greater East Asia Co-Prosperity Sphere, and probably a defensive struggle against the United States to maintain their hold on the region. A second operational stage also covered by the agreement was to "occupy or destroy as speedily as operational conditions permit," eastern New Guinea, New Britain, Fiji, Samoa, the Aleutians, Midway, and strategic points in the Australian area. According to historian John B. Lundstrom, this is as far as Japanese planning went.[108]

JAPANESE NAVY

The portion of the Japanese Navy which was to execute an attack on Pearl Harbor and provide cover and escort for the remainder of these operations had been preparing for its various roles for several weeks. It consisted of 10 battleships (BB), 6 cruisers, 112 destroyers (DD), and 65 submarines (SS). In addition, Japan had large numbers of auxiliary vessels, tenders, minesweepers, and escorts. The fleet was organized into nine naval stations in the homeland area, the China Area Fleet and the Combined Fleet. The Combined Fleet, which consisted of five mobile fleets (1st, 2nd, 6th , 1st Air Fleet, 11th Air Fleet) and three localized fleets (3rd, 4th, and 5th), was destined to carry the burden of the southern strategy as well as to conduct the strike on Pearl Harbor.[109]

In the opening campaigns of the first phase, the Combined Fleet was divided into four task forces: Force 1 was a carrier strike force consisting of all six fleet carriers, two battleships, and three cruisers under Admiral Chuichi Nagumo. It was to conduct a separate attack on Pearl Harbor. Force 2 , the South Seas Force (4th Fleet), extensively reinforced with land-based air units from Japan and submarines from the 6th Fleet, under Vice Admiral Shigeyoshi Inoue (CINC4), was to seize Rabaul, Wake, Guam, and Makin using a reinforced infantry regiment of 5,000 men (the South Seas Detachment). Force 3 consisted of fighting units from the 2nd and 3rd Fleets, the 11th Air Fleet, and the China

Admiral Isoroku Yamamoto, Commander-in-Chief, Combined Japanese Fleet

41

Area Fleet, under Vice Admiral Nobutake Kondo (CINC2), carriers from CarDivs 3 and 4, light and heavy cruisers and destroyers from the entire Combined Fleet, as well as hundreds of troop transports, supply vessels, escort vessels, and oilers, and the Southern Army under General Count Hisaichi Terauchi. It was to attack the Philippines, Thailand, and Malaya (the Kra Peninsula and Singapore). It was to follow up this with attacks on the Netherlands East Indies and Burma.[110] In addition to providing escort and cover for the Malay-Thailand invasion, the role of the 2nd Fleet included being Force 4, a "Distant Cover Force" for the forces invading the Philippines. Command of naval forces directly covering invasion of the Philippines was given to CINC 3rd Fleet, Vice Admiral Sankichi Takahashi.[111]

In addition to the vessels and their escorts, the Strike Force consisted of three submarines, I19, I21, and I23 on Ship Lane Patrol, 2DDs as Midway Neutralization Unit (presumably the same unit cited in the message of 16 November 1941, shown in Appendix A) and a train of eight tankers and supply ships.[112]

Details of the formation, training, and assembling of each of these Japanese naval elements (except for the Pearl Harbor Attack Force), as well as the supporting Japanese air elements involved in the Southern operations, were reported by the COMINT centers in Hawaii and Corregidor. Specifically, they observed Japanese air and naval forces gathering in the vicinity of Takao and Keeling on Formosa and Mako in the Pescadores, a group of islands between Formosa and China. They also noted Japanese assault forces gathering on Amami O Shima north of Okinawa and in the Palau Islands in the Mandates. Air support for the Philippine assaults was also seen assembling in the Palaus and on Formosa.

Because JN-25 messages as well as naval messages in other cryptsystems were largely unreadable, throughout the last few months of 1941 the messages were usually exploited for what their externals revealed (e.g., addresses, callsigns, association with others) and sent to Washington, where concentrated work on code and key recoveries was conducted. With some exceptions, the callsign change on 1 November seriously complicated the work of traffic analysis by introducing at the same time new procedures for addressing messages in which individual units were no longer called or addressed openly in the externals. (See Appendix C, note by COM-14 on 6 November.) Accordingly, when this practice was recognized, the record suggests that both COM-14 and COM-16, while still able to follow developments in the southern areas, had failed to establish continuity on the 1st Air Fleet callsign, which was noted and first identified on 3 November by COM-14 (see Appendix C). Moreover, COM-14 apparently neglected to review October traffic in which this fleet was also active and to make the correct associations regarding 1st Air Fleet organization. Regrettably, the record of Appendix A and Appendix C also suggests that between 1 and 17 November only message traffic which could be associated with pre-1 November southern area activity was examined even for its externals. The residue, including traffic pertaining to 1st Air Fleet activity, was apparently sent to Washington, which had no traffic analysis capability at this time and was concerned with only the cryptographic technicalities.[113]

Between early September and 4 December 1941, U.S. COMINT units at Pearl Harbor, Corregidor, and Guam intercepted and forwarded to Washington many thousands (26,581) of Japanese naval messages in the fleet general-purpose system (JN-25), a fleet minor-purpose system, a merchant vessel-navy liaison system, a merchant vessel-navy five-letter cipher, and a naval attaché cipher. Hawaii had no capability against JN-25, however, and because shortages of manpower in Washington precluded both code and cipher exploitation, none of these systems were read on a current basis even though Corregidor may have been nominally responsible for their exploitation.[114]

Had these messages been exploitable at the time, their stunning contents would have revealed the missing carriers and the identity of other major elements of the Strike Force.[115] Not only did the surviving messages (which were finally decrypted and translated in 1945 and 1946) provide the identity of the 1st Air Fleet's Strike Force, but they revealed the Strike Force's objective through analysis of its exercise activities and its movements prior to 26 November 1941. (See Appendix A.)[116]

The method of attack and objective of the Japanese Strike Force were revealed in messages intercepted between 21 October[117] and 4 November 1941.[118] On 21 October, Carrier Divisions 1, 2, and 5 began a series of exercises and training maneuvers which involved specially modified torpedoes.[119] These exercises, which probably ended on 6 November 1941, when CarDivs 1 and 2 were "to fire (torpedoes) against anchored capital ships" in Saeki Bay, amply demonstrated that the Strike Force had a naval objective.[120] Furthermore, the extraordinary measures taken by the Combined Fleet to insure adequate fuel supplies for the Strike Force demonstrated that the naval objective was at a distant point far removed from shore-based fuel and even beyond the normal Japanese resupply capability. Between 4 October and 1 December 1941, the Chief of Staff Combined Fleet, CINC 1st Air Fleet (commander Strike Force), units of the Strike Force, and many Japanese navy yards exchanged messages which revealed that three of the carriers (*Akagi, Soryu, Hiryu*) would carry fuel oil as deck cargo and in spare fuel tanks,[124] that additional oilers had been requisitioned into the Strike Force and modified for refueling at sea,[122] and that carriers and their escorts would conduct extensive practice of refueling while under way.[123]

By 12 November 1941, the carriers in the Strike Force had completed necessary repairs and had returned to their respective home ports or navy yards. Virtually all preparations for the Pearl Harbor assault had been completed. Two exceptions were the final deployment of the Strike Force to its point of departure, Hitokappu Bay in the Kuriles,[124] and completion of modifications to some oilers which were probably those involved in refueling the Strike Force on its return trip.[125] On 11 November 1941, however, CINC 1st Air Fleet issued a routine movement message containing a plan for anchoring at an unspecified future date CarDivs 1, 2, and 5 and several escort units and Maru (commercial) vessels in Saeki Bay in the Inland Sea.[126] There was no message confirming the fleet's arrival and, while it is entirely possible that not all elements of the Strike Force deployed to the Kuriles, the routine-appearing message, augmented on 1 December 1941 by deceptive radio broadcasts from Tokyo,[127] probably represented an attempt on the part of the Japanese to deceive U.S. monitors. Other Japanese naval messages now available clearly indicated that the Strike Force would be at sea by that date.

On 9 November 1941, the Commander Destroyer Squadron 1, a Strike Force unit (Chart A), while coordinating his activities with the Naval General Staff (NGS) Tokyo, sent a message which revealed that on 15 November 1941 Fleet carrier *Hiryu* of CarDiv 2 would be conducting a refueling drill off Ariake Bay while towing the *Kokuyoo* Maru.[128] In addition, examination of movement reports between 17 and 20 November 1941 reveals that the Strike Force flagship at that time was the battleship *Hiei* and that it was located at Hitokappu Bay (approximately 45-00N 147-40E).[129] Finally, on 19 November 1941 CINC Combined Fleet announced to all flagships a communication exercise on 22–23 November 1941, which excluded "the forces presently en route to the standby location."[130] Collectively, although not definitively, these messages strongly suggest that since 15 November 1941, instead of anchoring in Saeki Bay, major elements of the Strike Force had in fact been at sea probably moving to the high north latitudes of the Kuriles or, in the case of late departures, toward the east on the 30° line.

While the above information was not available at the time, daily traffic intelligence reports based on traffic analysis of communications of the Japanese Second, Third, and Fourth Fleets concerning events in the western and west-central Pacific areas were produced by both Hawaii and the Philippines. These reports were mailed to Washington where, after about two weeks en route, they formed the basis of biweekly OP-20-G summaries prepared for ONI.[131] Although the material was at times more than a month old, a factor which became critical in November and December 1941, officials in OP-20-G did have access to the same Japanese naval COMINT available to Kimmel at Pearl Harbor and Hart at Manila.

On occasion, such as on 26 and 27 November (see Appendix C), COM-14 and COM-16 COMINT summaries, because of their content, were sent to Washington as messages. These particular messages, though considerably less alarming than others issued by COM-14 during the October-November 1941 period, appeared at the same time as the famous "Winds" messages translations (see Appendix B) and contributed to the developing sense of crisis in Washington. Hawaii's report for 26 November 1941 was a comprehensive summary of the Japanese naval and air buildup assembling for a southern operation. It conveyed a distinct sense of alarm at events. Corregidor's report for 27 November identified in even greater detail the existence of both a Japanese Southern Force and a Mandates Force, including several Japanese ground force units (Base Forces) in the Mandates.

Hawaii's picture of the Japanese buildup was not as complete as it might have been, based on the details developed in their earlier summaries. COM-16's message confirmed and enlarged on COM-14's speculation regarding Japanese carriers in the Mandates (i.e., CarDiv 3, *Ryujo* and one Maru vessel). In a curious and unexplained reversal, however, COM-16 stated that COM-14's report could not be confirmed. It was also in this confusing context that COM-16 reassuringly and incorrectly reported that as of 26 November 1941 "all First and Second Fleet carriers are still in [the] Sasebo-Kure area." The two summaries from Hawaii and Corregidor on 26 and 27 November 1941, respectively, were thus unique not because of their imperfections but because they clearly showed Washington the current military situation in the Pacific as perceived by radio intelligence centers in the Pacific and Asiatic Fleets. It was entirely possible, as Layton later claimed, that the OPNAV warning message of 29 November 1941 was a direct result of the impact of these summaries on the Chief of Naval Operations. In view of the evidence, however, an even more likely possibility was that all the OPNAV warning messages of November were stimulated by COMINT: Japan's hostile intentions from the diplomatic messages and the likely targets from the daily COM-14 and COM-16 summaries which had inexorably found their way into the consciousness of official Washington.[132]

DIPLOMATIC MESSAGES

No review of the Navy's COMINT contribution to U.S. knowledge of Japanese pre-Pearl Harbor intentions would be complete without citing the benefits U.S. officials derived from the messages exchanged by Japanese diplomats in Washington and Tokyo. Although the credit for initial U.S. success against Japanese diplomatic machine systems must go to Army cryptanalysts, the Navy did play a significant role in providing collection and, after October 1940, in devoting the bulk of its cryptanalytic and linguistic resources to the exploitation effort. Unfortunately, as Safford had foreseen, the small Navy cryptanalysis effort in Washington was almost overwhelmed by the volume of messages from this source.[133] Little time and fewer resources were left over to attack JN-25, the code which, if read, would have provided operational details concerning the Japanese Strike Force.

As soon as possible after the Purple machines became available to Army and Navy cryptanalysts, the English texts of all translated diplomatic messages were delivered to both the Office of Naval Intelligence and the Military Intelligence Service (MIS) each day. By agreement, OP-20-GZ was responsible for dissemination of these messages within the Navy (Secretary of the Navy Frank Knox; CNO Admiral Harold R. Stark; A/CNO Admiral Royal E. Ingersoll; ONI, Admiral Theodore S. Wilkinson; and Chief, War Plans Division) and to the White House for the President's Naval Aide, Captain John R. Beardall.[134] Alwin D. Kramer and Arthur H. McCollum of the ONI Far East Desk decided what translations U.S. policymakers would see each day.[135] This arrangement was consistent with the dissemination rules laid down in the 1937 Orange War Plan. Similarly, MIS was responsible for dissemination within the War Department (Secretary of War Henry Stimson; Chief of Staff George C. Marshall; and Chief, War Plans Division) and to the State Department (Secretary of State Cordell Hull).

In Hawaii, neither the Army nor the Navy commander had facilities for decoding Japanese diplomatic messages. Overall policy regarding dissemination of Japanese intercept by both G-2 and ONI dictated that MAGIC material based on diplomatic messages would not ordinarily be distributed to any commander outside Washington. The

45

primary reasons for this policy were to protect the source and to retain in Washington the evaluation of purely diplomatic material. There was, however, no rule in either the War or Navy departments which prevented dissemination of MAGIC information to theater commanders. Facilities for decoding Japanese diplomatic messages, including messages in the Purple system (MAGIC), were available to Station C in the Philippines. However, if any diplomatic messages were read and translated there, it is possible that in the Asiatic Fleet diplomatic messages were not considered by themselves to be a likely source of either strategic or tactical warning.

WARNING MESSAGES

Warnings based, at least in part, on the contents of Japanese diplomatic messages were in fact sent to the Hawaiian and Philippine commands on at least three occasions, 24, 27 and 29 November 1941.[136] It seems clear, however, that after July 1941, as a matter of policy and probably as a practical security precaution, no intelligence material directly from MAGIC was sent to Admiral Kimmel in Hawaii or to U.S. command officials in the Philippines.[137]

Receiving the actual Japanese diplomatic messages would have done neither Kimmel nor Hart any practical service, aside from their obvious value in pinpointing vital areas of Japanese policies and intentions. They contained no Japanese naval or military information. Messages between Tokyo and Washington largely concerned the ongoing negotiations between Secretary of State Cordell Hull, Japanese Ambassador Kichisaburo Nomura, Minister Reijiro Wakasugi and, later, Saburo Kurusu, Japanese Ambassador Extraordinary. Messages between Tokyo, Washington, and other diplomatic posts frequently concerned Japanese espionage tasks and the efforts of diplomats to obtain information concerning U.S. naval and air dispositions in Panama, Hawaii, Manila, and various locations on the U.S. West Coast. Collectively, these messages conveyed an alarming interest in major fleet activity and an unmistakably hostile intention toward the United States. Their tenor deteriorated sharply after 26 November when the U.S. delivered its ten-point response to the Japanese note of 20 November. They did not, however, disclose the movements of the Japanese fleets.[138] Only the unread, untranslated Japanese naval messages held this vital information.[139]

Despite the fact that all messages in Japanese diplomatic channels were not available by 7 December and that the daily reports mailed from Hawaii and Corregidor were at least two weeks en route, by late November 1941 U.S. Navy officials in Washington, Pearl Harbor, and Manila well knew that war with Japan was imminent.[140] Made aware of hostile Japanese intentions by a profusion of intelligence (most of it COMINT), Admiral Stark, CNO, after 23 November 1941, repeatedly warned his Pacific commanders of impending Japanese attacks, placed restrictions on ship movements, and probably approved DNC's orders to destroy codes. The weight of evidence overwhelmingly favored Japanese air and naval strikes against the Philippines, and this locale actually appeared in the warning messages of 24 and 27 November as one of several likely Japanese objectives.[141]

REACTION

Inexplicably, the warnings issued by Washington were virtually the only direct military actions taken which can be traced directly to COMINT despite the sense of urgency that COMINT reflected. Admiral Kimmel in Hawaii, though a recipient of ample warning on the approaching crisis, was not particularly alarmed by COM-14's reports. Lacking any information on the Japanese 1st Air Fleet, and except for the warning messages, unaware of the content of messages in Japanese diplomatic channels, his attention was focused on the western Pacific.

With regard to the Philippines, the sense of alarm, at least in U.S. Navy circles, was paramount. By mid-September 1941, Admiral Thomas C. Hart, Commander in Chief Asiatic Fleet since July 1939,[142] had become very concerned over the intelligence reports on Japanese naval activities supplied by COMINT and other sources. By November, Hart clearly saw, through his regular visits to Station C in the Malinta Tunnel on Corregidor, that his fleet would soon be at war and that "time was running out."[143] Surviving records, however, do not provide a clear connection between a COMINT cause and an operational effect in the Asiatic Fleet.

Because of the general disagreement which prevailed among U.S. officials in Washington and the Pacific over U.S. objectives in the area, particularly with respect to British and Dutch possessions and the defense of the Philippines, Hart dispatched his fleet on a series of strategic deployments during September and October 1941 which first removed and then returned his forces to the Manila area. In September, convinced that the U.S. government would not defend the Philippines, Hart sent all his surface vessels to the south. On 27 October 1941, sensing a change in policy, Hart proposed to Washington that he join General Douglas MacArthur in defending the Philippines, and without first obtaining Washington's approval, he brought the Asiatic fleet back to Manila. On 20 November 1941, Washington disapproved his plan. This forced Hart, at virtually the eleventh hour, to redeploy his surface vessels to southern Philippine and Netherlands East Indies ports. Patrol aircraft and submarines were retained in the Manila area. Under these circumstances, it is difficult to distinguish Hart's deployments in response to intelligence from those taken in response to Washington.

Lacking a declaration of war by the United States against Japan and keenly aware that the United States did not wish to appear to be the aggressor, Hart, since receiving the first war warning from OPNAV on 24 November 1941, had been "edging toward increasingly risky action."[144] Based on "intelligence intercepts," Hart authorized air patrols over Japanese convoy movements along the China and French Indochina coasts. On 6 December 1941, after receiving confirmation that a Japanese amphibious force was steaming across the Gulf of Siam, Hart ordered one of his destroyer divisions to sail west from Balikpapan, Borneo, to Singapore. There the division commander was to place his ships under the British Fleet commander.[145]

Admiral Hart in his personal diary for the period 1-30 November indicated a preoccupation with two major problems: coordination of his own plans for defense of naval shore facilities with the U.S. air forces in the Philippines and Japanese troop movements along the China and Indochina coast. He estimated that the information provided him represented primarily a threat to Thailand and to the British in Indochina. He believed he had taken all prudent measures in anticipation of an attack, although his diary referred to no specific actions taken in response to the warning messages he received on 24, 27, and 29 November. On 7 December he wrote in his diary, "Guess war is just around the corner, but I think I'll go to a movie." The entry for 8 December states, accordingly, "It [the attack] was no surprise by a matter of 18 hours."[146]

Despite these rather tenuous indications of Hart's responses, there is plenty of evidence from another source that Hart did in fact react aggressively to Japanese activities. Japanese radio intelligence messages from Taiwan between 17 November and 3 December 1941, which were not read and translated until after the war in 1945-46, contained many reports of U.S. Army air and U.S. Navy air and ship reconnaissance. In addition, the Japanese consulate at Manila was very active in reporting the arrivals and departures of submarines and surface vessels.[147]

The Japanese perception of Army B-17 and fighter activity in the vicinity of Manila was one of declining activity. On 2 December 1941, Taiwan reported U.S. Army planes as "extremely inactive recently," and on 3 December as "greatly reduced since 30 November .... Prior to 30 November, 10 or more planes per day heard; on the 30th, 1; on the 31st, 2; none on the 3rd."[148]

U.S. Navy reconnaissance of the airspace around Luzon increased during November–December, according to Taiwan on 3 December 1941. Taiwan reported the area patrolled by aircraft on 2 December as "300 miles south and southeast of Manila and west of northern Luzon."[149] In addition, the U.S. Navy was also active in surface patrols in the vicinity of Taiwan, according to the Japanese messages.[150] In one of his many reports of visual observations, the Japanese consul in Manila, on 3 December 1941, reported departures from Manila of possibly seven submarines and, from Cavite, the departure of the light cruiser *Houston*, all to unknown destinations.

There is little doubt on balance that COMINT from Station C contributed to the Hart decision-making process. Certainly COMINT can claim a major share of the credit for the fact that on 8 December 1941 Asiatic Fleet losses were minimal, two amphibious patrol aircraft (PBY) and the gunboat *Wake*. Little if any of the COMINT provided by Station C came from cryptanalysis. Because Washington could not supply current code group meanings, Station C was not able to read messages in the Fleet General-Purpose System, JN-25, or in several of the minor naval codes. [151]

COMINT AFTER THE OPENING ATTACK

Following the attack on Pearl Harbor, COMINT resources in Hawaii, after a two-day pause probably caused by the loss of contact with Heeia, resumed publishing a daily COMINT summary. This summary continued to follow the activities of the Japanese Fleet. Corregidor concentrated its efforts on supporting local Navy and Army commanders by providing warning of incoming air strikes as well as supplying both CINCAF and CINCPAC information on the whereabouts of the Japanese Fleet.

At Pearl Harbor cryptanalytic emphasis shifted by mid-December from the Japanese Flag Officers Code and various shipping codes to recovering and exploiting the Japanese Fleet General-Purpose System. This was part of Safford's regrouping of tasks and responsibilities between Washington and Hawaii after the events of 7 December revealed with painful clarity the type of information probably contained in the Japanese Navy's messages and after the volume of diplomatic material declined. OP-20-G also recognized the tenuousness of its position in the Philippines and quickly put in motion plans to salvage Station C's manpower. Some of the senior officers in the communication directorate took this opportunity to centralize control of the entire COMINT operation in Washington.[152]

CONCLUSION

Throughout its relatively short life, OP-20-G, both in Washington and in the Pacific, had suffered a lack of manpower. In the final months of 1941, the lack of overall manpower resources combined with the disposition of the available cryptanalysts resulted in the failure to read the critical messages of the Japanese Strike Force targeted for Pearl Harbor. Briefly recapped, two thirds (fifty-three) of the officer cryptanalysts were in Washington where, if they were assigned to technical positions, they were exploiting Japanese diplomatic messages, operating a twenty-four-hour watch and performing code-room tasks which included running the Atlantic DF network, and conducting research on Japanese Navy cryptographic systems, e.g., JN-25. Less six officers in transit, the remainder were assigned in unequal proportions to Hawaii (twelve) and Corregidor (nine) where, in both stations, some were diverted to traffic analysis and machine room responsibilities. It may be argued that a more or less even distribution of collectors and DF operators between East Coast and Pacific stations was also a misalignment of critical resources, but it is clear that the placement and occupation of cryptanalytic personnel penalized Japanese Navy targets.

It is clear too that, between September and mid-November 1941, the activities of the Japanese Navy, as it prepared for war, were also overlooked by official Washington while it followed every fluctuation in the diplomatic negotiations between Ambassador Nomura and Secretary of State Hull. Judging from the conflicting guidance given to CINC Asiatic Fleet, abundant warning information produced by Hawaii and Corregidor from their analysis of the Japanese Navy's communications system and the activity it reflected was apparently either ignored altogether or treated as unsubstantiated rumor lacking any supporting evidence from readable messages. It is certain, however, that COMINT based on Japanese Navy communications available to these officials did not indicate that the Japanese intended to attack Pearl Harbor.

In an attempt to place some restraints in the path of the Japanese government, U.S. military leaders, with the approval of President Roosevelt, agreed with the British to establish separate commands for the Philippines and the Southwest Pacific; the former under Admiral Thomas Hart, CINC Asiatic Fleet, the latter under the direction of the senior British officer. The principal U.S. goals in the western Pacific at this time were to avoid being drawn into the British plans to defend Singapore and to avoid antagonizing the Japanese government. The U.S. claimed that these arrangements, along with the presence of the U.S. Pacific Fleet at Pearl Harbor, were sufficient deterrence but without representing a belligerent act.

Viewed in retrospect, these circumstances very strongly suggest that both OP-20-G and the Chief of Naval Operations had been swept along by the same overpowering pull of events in Europe and the Atlantic and were confused by conflicting American and European objectives in the Far East. Because of the unexpected German successes in 1940 and early 1941, the entire U.S. military establishment was confronted by an abrupt shift in both political and military priorities which, in January 1941, had become partially institutionalized by the first American-British Conference (ABC–1). This conference established the primacy of the Atlantic theater over all war planning. The decision to put the defeat of Germany in first priority ultimately led in June 1941 to cancellation of all war planning of any consequence in the western Pacific and placed naval emphasis on the western Atlantic and in the Pacific east of 180 degrees.

We will probably never know precisely why OP-20-G arranged its manpower resources in Washington and the Pacific as they were when the Japanese attacked Pearl Harbor and Manila. Undoubtedly, the new policies had left OP-20-G in an awkward position, creating new problems and aggravating old ones. Unwilling and perhaps unable to dismantle the COMINT edifice in the Pacific it had worked for twenty years to build, OP-20-G throughout 1941 let Hawaii and Corregidor perform the functions for which they had been prepared and trained while the work force in Washington did its best to provide support in both theaters as well as to abide by its odd-even agreement with the Army concerning Japanese diplomatic messages. The historical manpower problems generated at least in part by a lack of respect for the intelligence profession were probably felt most keenly in Washington, where a decentralized management philosophy had been unable to prevent a concentration of more work load than the work force could possibly achieve. The Washington center's limited cryptanalytic resources were not, moreover, focused on the Japanese Navy where they belonged. As a result, they could not read any of the Japanese Navy cryptographic systems, and they became preoccupied with the Japanese diplomatic targets, which were providing unprecedented exposure for Army and Navy COMINT centers at the highest levels of government. Without minimizing the influence of strong interservice rivalry, the fact that OP-20-G was not concentrating its resources on Japanese

Navy targets may suggest instead that a transition in emphasis toward the Atlantic by assigning more and more people to the twenty-four-hour watch had in fact already begun when the Japanese attack came.

Appendix A

Naval Messages Intercepted between
5 September and 4 December 1941

This appendix contains seventy-two selected Japanese naval messages intercepted between September and 4 December 1941 by Navy intercept sites at Hawaii, Guam, and Corregidor; these messages were not decoded and translated until September 1945–May 1946. At the end of the appendix are three diplomatic messages pertaining to the crisis which were translated on 8 and 30 December 1941. The Japanese naval messages are part of a total of 26,581 Japanese dispatches examined by U.S. Navy cryptanalysts.

The Japanese messages were originally discovered in a sanitized but unpublished group of 188 messages contained in a document obtained from the Navy Archives at Crane Indiana by the then NSA Historian, Mr. Henry Schorreck. Subsequently, some of the messages were located among approximately 2,400 translations given to the National Archives by NSA in 1978–79. Wherever this occurs, the appropriate reference number (SRN) is provided. Under these circumstances, it is not yet possible to verify in what Japanese cryptsystem each message was enciphered, nor have all the messages in the unpublished source been found in those released to the National Archives. (See particularly SRN-115202 to SRN-117840.)

It is interesting to note that the work of decrypting and translating these messages occurred at the same time that the congressional investigation of the attack on Pearl Harbor was being conducted. A review of the material provided witnesses before the congressional committee and to the committee itself by the Navy's Pearl Harbor Liaison Office, however, indicates that these messages were not made available to the Liaison Office. Ship identifications were taken from Conway's *All The World's Fighting Ships, 1922–46* (New York: Mayflower Books, 1980) and organizational relationships from *The Imperial Japanese Navy in WW II*, prepared in 1952 by U.S. Army, Far East Command, Military History Section.

The reader will note a 27 November 1941 message from Imperial Headquarters to the Striking Force containing the names of two Russian freighters, the *Uzbekistan* and the *Azerbaidjan*. The messages announced their presence in the Northern Pacific. Unhindered by restrictions of any kind, they were probably communicating with their owners in the Soviet Union. Their signals would have neatly supplied the basis for Seaman Z's sensational revelations that he had tracked the Japanese Striking Force's radio signals as it steamed toward Pearl Harbor. This episode is outlined in many secondary sources but most recently by John Toland and Edwin Layton in their books, *Infamy, Pearl Harbor and its Aftermath* and *And I Was There*, respectively.

5 Sep
From: COS2
To: 2nd Fleet
Info: COSCombined
"A state of complete readiness for battle operations must be achieved by the first part of November...exert even greater efforts toward achieving maximum fighting strength...."

9 Sep
From: COSCombined
To: All Fleet COS;
All Flt CINCs
"As conditions become more and more critical, each and every ship and unit will aim at being fully prepared for commencing war operations by the first part of November . . . completing all personnel changes ordered 3 August ASAP." SRN-115533

4 Oct
Between 4 October and 15 November the 1stAirFlt conducted almost daily drills at fueling at sea. The messages were most revealing in that their addressees actually showed the force structure of the Strike Force and their respective Trains (Tankers).

6 Oct
From: 1stAirFltStf
Action: CdrCarDiv2
CdrKagoshima Air Grp
In 1st Air Flt aerial torpedo attack drill #13, which was to be conducted on 21 October against BatDiv1, *Akagi* and *Kaga* were each allotted nine torpedoes and "*Sooryuu*" and "*Hiryuu*" are each allotted six torpedoes. SRN-117453

13 Oct
From: Staff Combined
To: All Flags
This message concerned the first Combined Fleet Communications drill. It contained the first references to a Striking Force and Advanced Expeditionary Force and mentioned dispatches suitable for X + 17, X + 30, and X + 45 days.

21 Oct
From: Tokyo Comms
To: ALLNAV
This message revised a Navy Call List by adding callsigns for new warships over a year before commissioning: the *Yamato* (BB) and the *Agano* (CL).

22 Oct
From: COS Sasebo SND
"Warship *Agano* launched ... today." SRN-116139

24 Oct
From: 1stAirFlt
Staff
To: Staff6FLT
Staff DesRon1,
Staff BatDiv3,
Staff CruDiv8,
1st Air Flt,
CarDiv4,
Tokyo ComUnit,
Tokyo DF Control,
StaffCombined
This message announced the second Combined Fleet Comm Test and again cited the
"Striking Force." Possible leading role for 1stAirFlt in Striking Force. SRN-117089

26 Oct
From: COS1stAir Flt
To: CruDiv8
DesRon1
SubRon1
This message requested that all ships scheduled to be assigned to the (Striking
Force?) have all torpedoes adjusted by 18 November. SRN-116684

27 Oct
From: COS1stAirFlt
Experience has shown that in operations the Train frequently preceded the Main Body.
Accordingly, Train-related messages were important. This message identified four
tankers to be assigned 1stAirFlt and to rendezvous at Sasebo by 10 November.

27 Oct
From: Staff1stAir Fleet
To: Staff BatDiv3
Message arranged torpedo launching exercise for CarDivs1/2/5.

28 Oct
From: COS1stAirFlt
[Three messages to and from 1stAirFlt reinforced idea that CINC1stAirFlt was
commander of Strike Force.] "On 30 October this Fleet will pick up from 5-10 (near
surface) torpedoes at Sasebo .... Classes on this torpedo will be held at Kanoya for about
five days from the 31st and then (emphasis) will be shifted to firing practice. By working
night and day it should be possible to complete 100 (attachments for torpedoes, probably
bow or stern planes) by 5 November." SRN-117301

28 Oct
From: COS1stAirFlt
"As the increase in the number of torpedoes handled and the lack of personnel is causing
grave delays in torpedo adjusting, please make special arrangements to send to this fleet
from Yokosuka Air Group – about 60 torpedo adjustment personnel to assist in the work of
adjusting torpedoes between the end of October and 20 November – 40 to Kanoya for
CarDivs1/2 – 20 to Ooita Air for CarDiv5 .... Please arrange increase of one torpedo
officer to each of the carriers in CarDivs1/2/5." SRN-116323

28 Oct

From: Yokosuka ND

"Send personnel and workers to carry out instructions on Type 91 torpedoes (equipped with stabilizers)...." SRN-116476

28 Oct

COS1stAirFlt

On 27 and 28 October arranged for two tankers to join his fleet by about 10 November – the *Shinkopu* Maru and *Toohoo* Maru. In the meantime these tankers were being equipped for refueling under tow.

30 Oct

From: COS1stAirFlt

Action: Kuroshia

Maru or Shinkoku Maru

Info: Kure NavyYrd

Kure Sanda Section

CdrCarDiv2, U/I

"When installation of gear for refueling undertow and preparations for action have been completed, *Kuroshio* (KOKU/CHOO) Maru and *Shinkoku* (KAMI/KUNI) Maru will depart Sasebo and Kure, respectively, on the 13th and proceed to Kagoshima Bay, conducting exercises with carriers en route. Request they load fuel oil for refueling purposes before they depart." SRN-116588

1 Nov

From: CINC1stAirFlt

"After completing battle preparations *Tooei* Maru will obtain about 750 drums of fuel oil (for use of *Akagi*) and 12,000 kerosene tins of fuel oil (for *Hiryu*) from Yokosuka . . . and rendezvous at Sasebo 10th . . . ." SRN-117150

1 Nov

From: CdrSubRon6

To: CINC2

". . . *Kinu* and *Yura* will ambush and completely destroy the U.S. enemy."
SRN-117001

2 Nov

From: Navy Minister

To: Yokosuka ND

"Have Air Depots 2 and 11 supply live bombs to *Akagi*, *Soryu*, *Hiryu*, *Shokaku*, and *Zuikaku* to ascertain their capabilities . . . ." SRN-117665

3 Nov

A message from the Chief of Naval Technical Bureau, General Affairs Section, to the Yokosuka, Sasebo, Kure, and Maizuru Yards emphasized that work on transport vessels be completed by 20 November.

3 Nov
From: Staff1stAirFlt
To: CdrSaekiAirBase
"In the 3rd Special Drill in ambushing, 54 shipboard bombers will carry out a bombing and strafing attack in sight of Saeki Base from 0815 on the 4th, 0715 on the 5th, and 0815 on the 6th, and about an hour or hour and a half afterwards 54 shipboard attack planes will carry out a similar bombing attack." SRN-117665

4 Nov
From: CdrCarDiv2
"CdrDesDiv23 will dispatch *Yuuzuki* (DD) to Saeki to arrive about 0700 the 6th. *Yuuzuki* will pick up and take to Kagoshima (4) torpedoes which CarDivs1/2 are to fire against anchored capital ships on the morning in question . . . ."

5 Nov
The equipment for refueling under tow at sea included special fenders .9mm in diameter, and the requisite lines for attaching them to the tanker. On this date a message listed 10 Maru vessels, at least five of which were firmly associated with the Striking Force. SRN-117031

5 Nov
In addition to refueling from tankers the Strike Force would be required to carry a deck cargo of oil drums. On carriers, the extra weight of the drums was cause for concern as shown by the following advice to COS 1st Air Fleet from the Chief, Bureau Military Affairs Section: "Regarding the loading of drums of fuel oil on ships of your fleet . . . it will affect the strength of the hull and the ship's performance.
A. Amount to be loaded: *Akagi*, under 600 tons; *Soryu* and *Hiryu* under 400 tons, and an equivalent weight will be removed.
B. In the case of *Akagi* and *Hiryu*, load amidships and avoid bow and stern.
C. In the case of *Soryu*, load evenly over length of ship.
D. We have prepared 1400 tons . . . ." SRN-116566

9 Nov
From: CINC1stAirFlt
From: CdrDesRon
The fact that major combat elements of the Strike Force were to be at sea on 13–14 November was revealed in two messages directing fueling at sea exercises for four Maru vessels with *Akagi*, DesRon1, CruDiv8, CarDiv2 and CarDiv5 and from CdrDesRon1 directing that the *Hiryu* and a tanker drill on the 15th off Ariake Bay (extreme southern Japan). SRN-115709, 115784

10 Nov
From: CINC6
To: 6thFltSubs
Info: AllFltCINCS
Maintain wartime radio silence on shortwave commencing 0000 November 11. SRN-117687

10 Nov
From: COSKureND
Info: COS1stAirFlt
"Arrangements have been made to (reequip) four Maru vessels for simultaneous port and starboard refueling by 13 November." SRN-117258

11 Nov
From: CINC1stAirFlt
This message assigned anchorages at Saeki Wan (western Inland Sea) to the capital ships and tankers of the Strike Force. SRN-115787

12 Nov
From: COS Combined Flt
Action: NavyTechBur Kure Navy Yrd
"In view of the necessity for completing by 17 November the installation for refueling at sea...." SRN-116589

12 Nov
From: CdrDesRon1
This message suggested that the entire Strike Force did not depart Inland Sea on 10 November: "In view of the scheduled operation of this unit it is desirable to complete loading of antiaircraft ammunition and fuses ... for *Abukuma*, (CL, DesRon 1 Flagship) DesDiv17, DesDiv15, and *Akigumo* (DD launched 4 November 1941 associated with Cardiv 5 by (13 November)...." SRN-115543

12 Nov
From: TokyoNGS Scty
To: SctyCombined
Info: Scty1stAirFlt
The following message seemed to firmly identify CINC1stAirFlt as Strike Force Cmdr: "Please supply the Striking Force with copies of the Special Area Designator List (issued by NGS) from those which have already been (secretly) issued to your headquarters." SRN-115381

14 Nov
From: Navy Minister
To: ALLNAV
"The publication Wartime Recognition Signals for Japanese Merchant Shipping will be placed in effect 1 December 1941...." SRN-115380

14 Nov
From: CdrCarDiv5
To: CINC1stAirFlt
"Flagship was changed to *Zuikaku* at 0830 on 14th ... 1st Section, *Zuikaku* and *Akigumo*; 2nd Section *Shokaku* and *Oboro*." SRN-115712

14 Nov
From: CINCCombined
To: 7 Marus
Message assigned 5 Maru vessels to CINCS1stAir, 2ndFlt, and 4thFlt. SRN-115785

15 Nov
From: Tokyo Bureau of Mil Prep
Message assigned *Akebono* Maru to 1st Air Flt.

16 Nov
From: CINC1stAirFlt
To: CdrDesDiv15
CdrDesRon1,
CdrSubRon1,
1stAirFlt(less CarDiv4, CarDiv3),
CdrBatDiv3,
Info: CINCSAllFlts
Tokyo DF Control
Hdg resolved question of who commands and composition of the Striking Force: "Strike Force OPORD#1: Commencing 0000 19 November, 'Battle Control' effective for short wave frequencies and 'Alert Control' for long wave." SRN-115397

16 Nov
From: SctyCombined
To: Flagships
Two messages revealed details of designator list and scope of forthcoming fleet operations: "Revision #1 to Navy Call list #9 effective November 15: Striking Force, Submarine Force (Southern Force), Maru Force, Communications Force, Commerce Destruction Force, Advance Expeditionary Force, Supply unit. . .(for each force), Southern Force, Northern Force, South Seas Force, E Force (British Malaya)*, H Force (Dutch East Indies)*, M Force (Philippines)*, Attached Force, G Occupation Force (Guam)*, AA Occupation Force (Wake)* and AF Destruction Units (Midway)* "(*ca 1942)."
SRN-115430, 116430

17Nov
From: Chief 1st Section NGS
To: COS1stAirFlt
Info: CdrBatDiv3
[The next seven messages were pivotal in locating the Strike Force.] *BB HIEI* was 1st section of BatDiv3.) "Suzuki (1776) is being sent to your Hq on board *HIEI* to report inspection results. " SRN-116436

18 Nov
From: Chief 1st Section, NGS
To: COS Ominato Guard District
Info: COS1stAirFlt
"Please arrange to have Suzuki (1776) who was sent to the 1stAirFlt on business, picked up at about 23 or 24 November at Hittokapu Wan by – of your command." (Hittokapu Wan is located in the Kurile Islands at about 45N-147-40E). SRN 116643. See also Prange, *At Dawn We Slept*, Ch 43, 342-52, for identity of Suzuki and his mission.

19 Nov
From: COS Ominato Guard District
To: NGS,1stSecCh
"He (Suzuki) will be taken aboard the *Kunajiri* (CA)." SRN 116920

19 Nov
From: CINC Comb Flt
To: All Flagships Combined Fleet
"The fourth series of communications tests for the Combined Fleet will be held as follows:
(on November 22 and 23). 2. Participating Forces: Combined Fleet (However, the forces
presently en route to the Standby Location will not receive test). 3. Principal topic for
consideration in this drill: Investigation and study of the communications setup required
to effectively handle the situation upon opening up of hostilities . . . ." SRN 115678 and
Prange, *At Dawn We Slept*, 332.

19 Nov
From: ProbSubUnit
To: CINCCombined,
CinC1stAirFlt,
CdrTokyoComUnit,
CdrYokosukaComUnit,
CINC6,
CdrOminatoComUnit
". . . until 2000, the 20th, Yokosuka Comm Zone. Until 0800, the 22nd, Ominato Comm
Zone. Thereafter, 1stAirFltFlagship Comm Zone." SRN 117673

19 Nov
From: ProbSubUnit
To: CINC1stAirFlt
CINC6
CdrTokyoComUnit
CdrOminatoComUnit
CdrYokosukaComUnit
". . . until 2000 the 20th Yokosuka Comm Zone. From 2000 the 20th until 0800 the
22nd,Ominato Comm Zone. Thereafter, 1stAirFlt flagship Comm Zone." (Ominato is
approx 41N–141E). SRN 117666/117674

20 Nov
From: StaffSubDiv2
To: CdrOminatoCom nit,
YokosukaComUnit,
Staff6FLT,
Staff1stAirFlt
"I-19 will leave Yokosuka Comm Zone on November 21, and enter Ominato Comm Zone.
At 1600 November 22 will enter 1stAirFleetFlagship Comm Zone." SRN 116329/116990.

20 Nov
From: CINCCombined
To: CINC2nd
CINC3rd
CINC4th
CINC11thAirFlt
CINC1stAirFlt
SaseboComUnit
Southern Expeditionary Fleet(Less SubRon/6)
". . . At 0000 on 21 November repeat 21 November, carry out Second Phase of preparations for opening hostilities." SRN-115385

20 Nov
From: CINC11thAirFlt
To: 11thAirFlt
"Commencing 20 November, when planes (or plane units) are shifted, maintain precautionary shortwave silence."

20 Nov
From: Hainan Guard District
To: Hainan Force Staff
"Report of leakage of secret information regarding the concentration of our troops on Hainan Island to a foreigner. Commencing 24 November no one will be permitted to leave or enter Hainan Island . . . ." SRN-115438

20 Nov
From: Shiriya
Action: COSCarDivs, Combined Flt
"1. Will complete loading fuel oil (aviation gasoline) and other miscellaneous equipment 21 November. 2. The main generator and other minor repairs will be completed 23 November. 3. Expect to get underway on the 24th and join up during morning of 27 November. 4. Striking Force Secret Operation Order #6 has not been received." SRN-115375

21 Nov
From: Navy Minister
To: All Majcoms Afloat
[Radio calls are normally effective for about six months. The last change was on 1 November. The following message is noteworthy.] "Commence using Call List #10 from 1 December and discontinue using List #9 as of 30 November."

21 Nov
From: C.O.Shiriya
To: CdrDesDiv7
"We are now undergoing overhaul at Yokosuka. Expect to depart November 24 and arrive Sea on November 27. Advise rendezvous point with your unit. Regard fueling at sea ...." (DesDiv7 is escort of CarDiv1, *Akagi* and *Kaga*)

22 Nov
From: PossCarDiv4
Kasuga Maru and *Hokaze* (DD) CarDiv4 ordered to transport planes from Sasebo to Palau ASAP.

25 Nov
From: Chief, 1st Section, Naval Sec, Imperial Hq
The Japanese had maintained a close interest in the U.S. Marines at Shanghai and Tientsen for several weeks and knew they would be evacuated on the American liners *President Madison* and *President Harrison*. This message ordered COS China Area Fleet to report time of departure by urgent dispatch to 2nd and 3rd Fleets, 2nd China Expeditionary Fleet and Bako Guard District. See SRN 116737, 27 November.

25 Nov
From: COS2
To: COSCombined
Info: COS3
". . . Since we have assigned all eight patrol boats to the Philippine Force and orders for their use have already been issued . . . ." SRN-116910

25 Nov
From: CINCCombined
To: All Flagships
"From 26 November, ships of Combined Fleet will observe radio communications procedure as follows:
1. Except in extreme emergency the Main Force and its attached force will cease communicating . . . ." SRN-116866

25 Nov
From: Imperial Hq,
1stSecNavSecCh
To: COS2,
COS3,
COS4,
COS11th Air,
COSSEF,
COSChina Area Fleet,
All ND COS
"(Plans) for exhaustive conscription of . . . and civilians are in hands of Central Authorities. In order to preserve security, however, they will be activated at a future time
. . . ."
SRN-116908

26 Nov
From: COS2
Anticipating casualties the Navy arranged for hospital facilities for the end of December. "Complete all necessary arrangements for the hospitalization of 1,000 patients each at Bako (including Takao), Sama, and Palau . . . . Be prepared to supply ten times the annual 'battleship requirements' of medical supplies for dressing of wounds and disinfection by 10 February 1942." SRN-115439

26 Nov
From: ComCarDiv3
To:CINC2
Info:CINC3
"In view of this force's operations and future we definitely desire to be refueled before arriving at Palau . . . ."

27 Nov
From: 1stSecNavSec
Imperial Hq.
To: Striking Force
COSCombined
"Although there are indications of several ships operating in the Aleutians area, the ships in the Northern Pacific appear chiefly to be Russian ships . . . . They are *Uzbekistan* (about 3,000 tons . . . 12 knots) and *Azerbaidjan* (6,114 tons less than 10 knots). Both are westbound (from San Francisco)." SRN-116667

27 Nov
From: TokyoComUnit
To: All Fleets
From: 1stSecNavSec
Ch,Imperial Hq
To: Striking Force,
COSCombined
"1. Weather report. The low pressure center of 740mm which was near 'N RI 0 Na' today at noon, is advancing at a speed of 45km. Wind speed is over 15m, within 1000km to SW of center and about 26m near the center. The high pressure center in "RU" area continues to proceed eastward at a speed of 45km. 2. Prince Hiroyasu Fushimi sends the following msg to CINC Nagumo: 'I pray for your long and lasting battle fortunes.' " SRN-116668

27 Nov
From: Navy Minister
To: All Majcoms,
CINCall NDs,
CINC All Guard Districts
"From now on all merchant shipping, all Naval Comm units, and Naval Shipping will stand radio guard (Listening watch) as set forth in Articles 12 and 13 of Secret Communication Regulations for Merchant Shipping." SRN-115636

28 Nov
From: Imperial Hq.
NGS
To: All Majcoms
"Beginning 1 December 1941, Tokyo Comm Unit will initiate broadcasts on . . . 4175kc in order to (maintain) volume of traffic . . . afloat, etc., in accordance with principles given in 2nd Communications Analysis of 1941."

28 Nov
From: Ch1stSec,Nav
Sec, Imperial Hq.
To: All Majcoms,
All NDs,
All Guard Dist,
Tokyo Hydro office
"Commencing this date, in special weather reports sent from (this office) locations will be
indicated by Navy Grid Chart – afloat weather list." SRN-115456

28 Nov
From: Ch1stSec,Nav
Sec, Imperial Hq
To: Striking Force
"At noon on the 28th a high pressure area of _ mm located in 'TSU' and 'HE' sectors moving
ESE . . . 55kmh. Another high pressure center of about the same pressure in 'U' sector is
almost stationary . . . ." SRN-115690

29 Nov
From: CINC4
"All capital ships, destroyers, submarines of the South Sea Force and the *Kujokawa* Maru
are to maintain battle condition short wave silence, starting 1200 Nov 29." SRN-115435

29 Nov
From: (6thBasFor)
To: CdrGdDiv#52
CdrGdDiv53
Info: DesRon6
Cdr4th lt
"The following forces are to be added to the special landing forces for the "U" Occupation
Operations . . . ." SRN-115396

30 Nov
From: COSBakoGuardDist
Action: COSCombFlt
COS2ndFlt
COSSouthChinaFlt
"At 0200 the 30th, auxiliary gunboat *ASO* Maru observed three American minesweepers
(650tons) of _ class at point 10 miles on a northeasterly course. In reference to _ #81, it is
believed that the Pescadores and Takao areas are being reconnoitered. We are attempting
to confirm these movements." SRN-117290

30 Nov
From: ChTokyoComOf
To: Striking Force
Info: COSCombined
"At noon on the 30th, a high pressure area of _ mm located in "YU," "RE," "TSU," "HO,"
"U" blocks with other areas quiet on the whole . . . . conditions will continue for about two
more days. At 0900 on the 30th there was a five meter west wind in AI (Oahu*) and rain at
AF(Midway*)." (*ca 1942) SRN-115460

1 Dec
From: COSSaseboND
To: CdrOkinawa
Area Base Force
"We have received word from Naha customs that the Philippine registered ship KUROBEERUGOO (kana) (44-ton) arrived in Naha on 30 Nov. Seal her radio at once – delay departure of this ship – prevent their learning of our activities." SRN-117693

1 Dec
From: Shiriya
To: ComDesDiv7
"This ship is proceeding direct to position 30-00N, 154-20E. Expect to arrive that point at 1800 on 3 Dec. Thereafter will proceed eastward along the 30 degree North latitude line at speed of 7 knots." SRN-115398

2 Dec
From: CINCCombined
To: Combined Flt
"This dispatch is Top Secret. This order is effective at 1730 on 2 December. Climb NIITAKAYAMA 1208, repeat 1208." (Climb Mount Niitaka December 8) SRN-115376 (In late 1945, possibly with knowledge in hand that this message was stipulated in Flt OPORDER#1, its meaning is understood by OP-20-G to be, "Attack on 8 December." In the congressional investigation this message was incorrectly reported as sent on 6 December 1941. (Hearings Part 1, 185))

2 Dec
From: NavMinister
To: All ND CINCS
All GD CINCS
All Fleet CINCS
"Starting 4 December 1941, system #8 of Naval Code will be used and system #7 discontinued. (List 7 will still be used with some Japanese stations.)" SRN-116741

2 Dec
From: Tokyo (Togo)
To: Honolulu
[In connection with the CarDiv2 message of 4 November 1941 regarding preparations to fire torpedoes against anchored capital ships, the following message in a naval attaché system was particularly noteworthy. This message was received in Washington on 23 December 1941 and translated by the Army on 30 December 1941. (Connorton, Appendix 1, 194, item 87)] "In view of the present situation the presence in port of warships, airplane carriers, and cruisers is of the utmost importance. Hereafter, advise me whether or not the warships are provided with anti-[torpedo] nets."

3 Dec
From: CINCCombined
To: Combined Flt
"From 0000, Dec 4th change ship frequency system to #1 . . . ."

5 Dec

From: BurMilPrep, Tokyo

To: NavAttaché, Washington, Mexico

[Only one message was found after 0000 4 December 1941 in the old cipher which could have been read before 8 December.] "Copy being sent by wire to Naval Attaché London. Dispose of the Cipher Machine and all of its rules for use at once."

6 Dec

From: Honolulu

To: Tokyo

[Regarding the torpedo net message of 2 December in diplomatic channels the following was translated by the Army on 8 December 1941]: ". . . in my opinion the battleships do not have torpedo nets . . . ."

Appendix B

Summary of Diplomatic Messages
July – November 1941

After 24 November 1941, events in U.S.-Japanese diplomatic negotiations moved very swiftly to their climax on 7 December. A number of important diplomatic messages passed between Tokyo and Washington between July and November; these are summarized below. These early messages and those exchanged after 24 November which have been selected for inclusion in this appendix are so revealing that it is easy to lose sight of the fact that U.S. officials were often reading these messages at about the same time as the Japanese diplomats. The "War Warning" messages sent by OPNAV beginning on 24 November have also been included in this appendix to insure that the reader fully appreciates their correlation with events occurring in diplomatic circles.

- Despite changes in its government, Japan remained committed to the Tripartite Pact with Germany and Italy.

- Japan frequently expressed determination to use force against the United States and Great Britain.

- Japan established an espionage network in the United States.

- Plans for evacuation of Japanese diplomatic, espionage, and newspaper personnel were discussed.

- Germany and Italy applied pressure on Japan to provoke war with the U.S.

- Japanese attitude toward the U.S. Open Door policy hardened after 16 October when Tojo took over the government. Japan wanted the U.S. to approve Japanese policies in the Far East – including China and French Indochina – and restore Japanese trade status with the U.S.

- Ambassador Nomura's attempt to resign on 22 October was refused.

- On 4 November, Ambassador Saburo Kurusu, sent to help Nomura, was not optimistic that negotiations would be successful. He arrived in Washington on 17 November.

- On 5 November Tokyo established a 25 November deadline for completion of negotiations.

- Nomura reported on 10 November on statements from high-ranking politicians and cabinet members (a) that the U.S. was not bluffing, (b) that it was ready for war, (c) that it had reliable reports that Japan would be on the move soon, and (d) that the president and secretary of state believed these reports.

- On 19 November 1941, two messages from 15 November were read which discussed plans to evacuate Japanese citizens from the U.S.

The messages which follow are arranged in order of transmission. Army messages are indicated with an "A" and Navy messages with an "N." The date given is the date the message was translated.

N   25 Nov   A circular message from Tokyo to Washington on 15 November with detailed instructions on how to destroy code machines.

N   28 Nov   A circular message from Tokyo to Washington on 19 November with detailed instructions to listen for "Winds Execute" messages to be added to Japanese news broadcasts in case of diplomatic emergencies involving the U.S., England, or Russia. When heard, embassies were to destroy all codes, papers, etc.

N   26 Nov   A circular message from Tokyo to Washington on 19 November, sent after above message but translated earlier, contained instructions to listen for an abbreviated "Winds" message in general intelligence broadcasts repeated five times at beginning and end, i.e., only the word *East, West,* or *North* would be spoken five times.

A   28 Nov   Circular message from Tokyo on 20 November said U.S.-Japanese situation would not "permit any further conciliation by us" and rejected all feelings of optimism.

A   22 Nov   Tokyo informed Washington on 22 November that, by 29 November if agreement had not been reached, "things are automatically going to happen."

       24 Nov   OPNAV message warned of possible Japanese "aggressive movement" toward Philippines, Guam, or any direction.

A   26 Nov   Tokyo message to Washington on 26 November contained telephone brevity code to be used because "telegrams take too long." The code covered topics under negotiation, situations, and personalities.

       27 Nov   OPNAV WAR WARNING message.

A   29 Nov   Message on 26 November from Nomura to Tokyo recommended that Japan break diplomatic relations with the U.S. in a formal manner rather than "enter on scheduled operations" without prior announcement particularly since "our intention is a strict military secret." A formal break would avoid responsibility for the "rupture."

N   2 Dec   A circular message from Tokyo on 27 November contained another brevity code in which codewords were assigned specific meanings, e.g., "Japan's and USA's military forces have clashed" equals, "HIZIKATA MINAMI."

N	28 Nov	A telephone conversation on 27 November between Washington (Kurusu) and a foreign office official in Tokyo named Yamamoto. Tokyo used telephone code to convey a message referring to an attack on the U.S.
	29 Nov	OPNAV WAR WARNING message. Text indicated Army had also been notified.
A	1 Dec	Message from Tokyo to Berlin on 30 November directed the Japanese ambassador to inform Germany that U.S. relations had ruptured and that "war may break out quicker than anyone dreams." Regarding Russia, Tokyo stated that if Russia reacted to her move southward and joined hands with England and the U.S., Japan was "ready to turn on her with all our might." Tokyo requested the Germans and Italians to maintain "absolute secrecy."
N	1 Dec	Message from Tokyo to Washington discussed means of allaying U.S. suspicions regarding Japanese reactions to the U.S. proposal of 26 November. News media were to be advised that "negotiations are continuing." A plan was discussed to make a formal presentation in Washington vice Tokyo. The message queried president's reaction to Tojo's bellicose speech.
N	1 Dec	A circular message from Tokyo on 1 December advised Washington that London, Hong Kong, Singapore, and Manila had been instructed to destroy code machines.
	2 Dec	OPNAV instructed CINCAF to establish defensive patrols.
A	4 Dec	Message from Rome to Washington on 2 December said that Tokyo believed the Hull note of 26 November "absolutely unacceptable," and "a conflict(?) in the near future is considered very probable." Rome also said Tokyo believed American Navy in Pacific was "not strong enough for decisive action."
N	3 Dec	Message from Tokyo to Washington on 2 December instructed Washington to burn all codes except one copy of the codes being used in conjunction with the machine (i.e., PURPLE), the O Code, and the abbreviation code. Washington was also to burn messages, other secret papers, and telegraphic codes, and possibly to destroy one machine.
	3 Dec	An OPNAV message regarding Japanese instructions to burn codes.
N	6 Dec	Messages from Berlin and Rome to Tokyo on 3 December described Japanese attempts to obtain German and Italian assurances that they would follow the Japanese declaration of war on the U.S. with their own. Hitler was not available, but Mussolini agreed.

	4 Dec	OPNAV ordered U.S. codes destroyed.
N	6 Dec	Washington confirmed destruction of codes on 5 December.
N	6 Dec	Tokyo message on 5 December ordered four individuals in Washington to leave immediately. The translation contained a note which identified one as head of Japanese espionage in the Western Hemisphere and the others as his assistants.
A	6 Dec	Tokyo message to Washington on 6 December alerted Nomura that a formal reply to the 26 November note had been prepared, was very long, and would be in 14 parts.

The messages quoted in this appendix are taken from Radio Intelligence Publication Number 87Z, "The Role of Radio Intelligence in the American-Japanese Naval War," Vol. I, Section A, by Ensign John V. Connorton, USNR. SRH-012, RG 457.

Appendix C

Highlights from COM-14 Daily COMINT Summary

This appendix represents abstracts taken from the daily COMINT summaries published by COM-14. To aid the reader in correlating these highlights with actual daily events, I have included salient extracts from Morison's *History of U.S. Naval Operations*. To show the correlation between COMINT and warnings issued by Washington, I have also inserted, at the appropriate times, diplomatic and OPNAV messages.

The sources are indicated as follows:

"S" indicates COM-14 Traffic Intelligence Summaries, July–December 1941, SRMN-012.

"C" indicates Radio Intelligence Publication Number 87Z, *The Role of Radio Intelligence in the American-Japanese Naval War*, Volume I, by Ensign John V. Connorton, USNR (SRH-012).

"M" indicates Volume III, *The Rising Sun in the Pacific, 1931–April 1942*, by Samuel Eliot Morison.

Edited copies of the COM-14 Daily Summaries for the period 1 November–6 December 1941 may also be found in PHA, Part 17, 2601–42.

S	16 Jul	Combined Air Force concentration in Takao [Taiwan] included in 3rdFlt addresses. Indications it will move south, i.e., to Taiwan from Japan. 4thFlt concentrating in Mandates [Defense?)] *Hiryu* and probably other carriers concentrating in Taiwan area "awaiting the assumed Southern Operations."
S	31 Jul	New Task Force Formed – CINC3 , China Flt, South China Flt.
S	20 Aug	AirRon4 move indicated by heavy traffic.
S	21 Aug	Commander AirRon24 at Saipan.
S	24 Aug	New carrier, *Shokaku* – appeared in traffic. [Confirmed by COM-16 on 28th.]
M	Sep	Training by carriers and air groups for Pearl Harbor attack began in September.
S	8 Sep	New carriers *Shokaku* and *Zuikaku* being fitted out. [The *Shokaku* completed fitting out on 8 August 1941, the *Zuikaku* on 25 September 1941.] Plane complements for all carriers are being completed.

S	12 Sep	COM-16 [confirmed] a new force being organized, possibly a 5thFlt.
S	18 Sep	Heavy air-related traffic suggests air movement into Mandates forthcoming.
S	22 Sep	*Ashigara* relieved by *Isuzu* as Flag of South China Flt. [*Isuzu* is Flag of DesRon5/3rdFlt.]
S	23 Sep	Task Force being formed out of elements of 1st /2ndFlts.
S	24 Sep	Additional carrier division organizing. [The *Shokaku* and *Zuikaku* later became CarDiv5.]
S	26 Sep	Preparations noted for large-scale 1st/2ndFlt exercises with carrier divisions.
S	28 Sep	Preparations may indicate possible hostile action.
S	1 Oct	2ndBasFor [3rdFlt] to board ship [possibly Flagship 3rdFlt] at Sasebo leaving some units behind.
S	2 Oct	COM-14 says, "3rdFlt being built up to its French Indochina composition."
S	4 Oct	Volume of traffic since callsign change indicates reorganization. COM-16 agrees that flag of CINC Combined Flt shifted to *Mutsu* [BatDiv1/1stFlt] and Flag CINC2 is in *Maya* (CruDiv4, 2nd section, 5thFlt).
M	5 Oct	Carrier air groups officers told Pearl Harbor their objective. Training continued.
S	9 Oct	Yokohama Air Corps addressed message to Taiwan addressee. Chitose Air and AirRon24 to move to Mandates soon. Naval Auxiliaries in Mandates continue to increase, now 33.
S	11 Oct	Chitose Air moving to Saipan without commander. Yokohama Air at Truk as is commander AirRon24. Large air unit appears at Hainan and Kanoya. Large air movements noted in 4thFlt.
S	12 Oct	Commander Yokohama air at Kwajalein.
S	14 Oct	Movements to Mandates noted by Yokohama, Chitose, and Yokosuka Air units.
S	15 Oct	5thFlt is formed.

S   16 Oct   Communications network is expanding particularly in air-related communications. Callsign usage same as for "Temporary Shore" or "Advanced Base" stations associated with South China, Indochina campaigns.

S   16 Oct   CINC Combined Fleet may have returned to Nagato. Associated with 1st/2ndFlts, carriers, and subs. Chitose Air en route Mandates, Yokohama Air at Truk, Yokosuka Air possibly Palau area. Evidence that Navy is taking over Maru vessels and issuing callbooks and organizing into units.

S   17 Oct   Tokyo relayed message from Spratly Island [South China Sea] to Takao [Taiwan] under priority procedure to COS Combined Flt, ComCarDiv4, CarDiv4, Intel unit Bako (Taiwan), COS South China Flt, COS French Indochina Force (Southern Exped. Force), Resident Naval Officer (RNO) Taihoku [Taipei], Cdr 11th Air Corps [sic] [Fleet], and COS South China Air Force. [COM–14 confused over whereabouts of CINC Combined and status of *Mutsu* as Flagship.] During last week September *Mutsu* joined 2nd Flt after stint at yard at Kure. On 1 Oct, CINC2 "relieved as CINC Combined and hoisted flag on *Mutsu*." On 17 October, CINC2 retransmitted message originated on 14th addressed as follows: Action: 2ndFltColl, 3rdFltColl, Combined AF, SubRon5, SubRon6, AirRon7, BatDiv3; Info: ComCarDivs, CINC Combined, Radio Takao, Radio Palao, Radio Tokyo. A total of 38 Naval Auxiliaries in Mandates.

S   18 Oct   CINCChinaFlt replaced; date unknown. Appears to be heavy air movement between Empire and Mandates.

S   19 Oct   Guam reports 13 new Naval Auxiliaries in Mandates. [Hawaii and Philippines disagree over callsign for a new carrier – either *Zuikaku* or *Shokaku*.]

S   21 Oct   Japanese DF traffic first noted on 20 October is increasing. Stations at Chinkai, Manchukuo area, Chosen area, Jaluit, Sasebo. Combined Air Force sent message which included carriers in addresses. COM-14 notes this not normal and that scope of addees indicates a large-scale operation over a long distance. Action: Navy Minister, Chief Naval General Staff (NGS), Combined Air Force, CarDiv4 less HOSHO and U/I, CarDiv3; Info: CINC China Flt, CINC South China Flt, all major Fleet Flagships.

S   22 Oct   11 Maru vessels noted using suffix denoting "C.O. Naval Detachment Aboard" in connection with Takao/Hainan air movement. A 5thFlt continues to appear. The "Special Task Force" or "Southern Expeditionary Force" [SEF] [Flag in *Kashii*] associated with CarDiv4 in future operations. Impression grows that a large-scale operation is in progress in Mandates, in Takao/Hainan/Indochina areas and in Kuriles.

S	23 Oct	COM-14 noted message from DF Hq Tokyo to collective addressee which omitted CINC South China Force but included SEF, "a circumstance reminiscent of Indochina operations when 3rdFlt assumed major importance with CINC South China Force in subordinate role."
S	24 Oct	2ndFlt sent message to unusual action addressees not normally under 2ndFlt and information addressees which give southern flavor to whole group. Action: 3rdFltColl, CombinedAirColl, 2ndFltColl, BatDiv3, DesRon3; Info: Palao; Spratly/Cam Ranh; DF; Tokyo; CINC Combined; ComCarDiv5.
S	24 Oct	Communications Officer CarDivs message to following addressees: BatDiv3, CruDiv8, CarDivs less CarDiv3; Info: Tokyo Radio, U/I addressee, Communications Officer Combined Flt. [Major units of Pearl Harbor Strike Force. See Appendix A, same date, for related messages.]
S	26 Oct	U/I Air Command to move from Taiwan to South China. 5thFlt becoming more tangible at Yokosuka.
S	28 Oct	COS French Indochina Force aboard Flagship Combined Fleet. Indications growing that 4thFlt is preparing for operations. CINC4 sending traffic to Combined Flt, Subs, CarDivs, and Tokyo addressees.
S	30 Oct	Tokyo ComDiv message volume unprecedented. Possible communications change in offing COM-14 believes movement of 3rdFlt imminent. Station C reports *Ashigara* departed for South. New carrier [*Koryu*] associated with Saipan, Truk, and Yokosuka Air suggesting move to Saipan soon.
S	31 Oct	Japanese Navy callsigns changed in Fleet and Air units. Commanders 11 and 12 Air Corps [sic], Shiogama Air in Takao area. COM-14 noted similarity to concentration at Hankow Air, July–August.
S	1 Nov	All major fleet callsigns recovered. Shore callsigns no change. Individual callsigns slow to collect and recover.
S	3 Nov	General messages continued to emanate from Tokyo in unprecedented numbers. Numbers not understood now that communications change past. COM-14 suggested that messages were reports of some kind. A new addressee reading 1stAirFlt noted for first time. This is a new organization. Possibly explains association between CarDivs3 and 4 and Combined AF, i.e., between shore-based and Fleet Air. [See Appendix A, 4 October and 6 October, for earlier appearances of 1stAirFlt address.]
S	6 Nov	Tokyo radio now using "general" or "area" calls vice unit calls and may have eliminated address and originator from messages on broadcast circuits. Very heavy air concentration on Taiwan includes the entire Combined Air Force-Commander and Staff, one carrier division, and the Fleet Air Arm.

S	7 Nov	Possible heavy concentrations in Marshalls causing congestion on Mandates circuits.
S	8 Nov	Formation of Force in Takao/Bako area [Taiwan] under Cdr Combined Air nearly completed based on reports addressed to CINC Combined Flt; Naval Ministry; CdrCarDivs; Combined Air; 1stFlt, and Shore addressees associated with movement or organizational changes. Force possibly includes CarDivs3 and 4 plus Auxiliaries, and units of Combined Air and 1stFlt. Uncertain area of operations.
C	8 Nov	Details of U.S. aircraft in Philippines sent to Tokyo by Manila on 1 November.
S	9 Nov	COS SEF in Tokyo.
M	10 Nov	Japanese Army and Navy agree to attack plan. Pearl Harbor Strike Force departs home waters for Kuriles. [See Appendix A.]
S	10 Nov	Combined Flt mostly in Kure area, BatDiv3, CINC2, and two CruDivs noted specifically. 3rdFlt in Sasebo/Takao; 4thFlt in Truk; 5thFlt has one unit at Chichi Jima; CdrCarDiv3 possibly with Combined Flt units at Kure/Sasebo; CINC Combined AF at Takao.
C	12 Nov	Messages from Tokyo to Manila on 5 November request information regarding aircraft and ships.
S	12 Nov	CarDiv3 returned to Kure from Takao per COM-16.
S	13 Nov	Activity of BatDiv3 unclear – Flag at sea, Cdr in Yokosuka, DivComOfficer active with Truk, Saipan, Palao – other ships in Div unlocated. One CruDiv of 2ndFlt in traffic with Palao, possibly in that area. Other units of 1stFlt seem inactive. Carriers inactive.
S	14 Nov	4thFlt Staff members in Tokyo. Carriers remain in home waters with most in port. Flag of BatDiv3 heard. DesRon3 and CruDiv7 of 2ndFlt active, may proceed south.
S	15 Nov	Combined Fleet to BatDiv3, DesRons1/3, associated with SEF. CINC2 most active – appears to be arranging operations of units involving 1st/2ndFlts, carrier and air units. Purpose of air concentrated in Takao area unknown; possibly will move south to SEF.
S	16 Nov	1st/2ndFlt units remain in Kure area. CINC2 has assumed an important role involving units of several fleets, SEF, Combined Air, CarDivs and Mandates fleet. DesRon1 is operating with CarDivs and BatDiv 3.
C	18 Nov	OPNAV sent messages to CINCAF regarding Japanese patrols from Mandates and Dutch concerns/intentions regarding Japanese buildup in Mandates which also threatens Netherlands East Indies.

S	18 Nov	CINC Combined Flt active sending and receiving messages. CINC2/SEF/Combined AF association very plain in messages sent and received. BatDiv3, CarDivs, two DesRons associated in traffic. CINC2 in command of large Task Force comprising 3rd Fleet, Combined AF, some CarDivs, and BatDiv3. No movement from home waters has been noted. 3rdFlt will move from Sasebo in near future. 2ndBasFor may be transporting air units or equipment.
S	20/21 Nov	Unusually heavy traffic Tokyo to all Majcoms. NGS urgent precedence to COS South China Flt. Personnel Bureau sending long personnel messages. DF traffic heavy. Tokyo/Takao circuit forced into duplex to handle traffic. Combined Fleet: Flags of 1st/2ndFlts in Kure area. Most of both Flts in Kure/Sasebo area. BatDiv3 still in Yokosuka area. Traffic to and from CINC2 abnormally high; association with CINC3 continues. Partial list of forces being assembled by CINC2 in two days (27 units, 11 Marus) includes CarDiv3, AirRons6/7; CruDivs5/7; DesRons3/4/5; BasFor1/2; Shiogama Air Corps; possibly two additional air units; and 13 U/I units. Mandates/4thFlt: Palao seen as locale for forthcoming concentration of forces based on communications activity. Concentration in Marshalls far greater than Palao.
M	22 Nov	Pearl Harbor Strike Force completes move to Kuriles.
S	23 Nov	High precedence traffic increasing. Typical headings are (a) from Tokyo Address to Collective Shore; Info: COS Combined, 1st/2nd/3rd/4th/5thFlts, SEF; (b) from COS3 to COS2; Info: COS Combined AF, SEF; (c) from Tokyo to COS3 and SEF; Info: Sama, Hainan; (d) from U/I Flt unit to Radio Takao and Hainan, U/I Flagship; Info: Radio Tokyo and 2ndFlt Flagship; and (e) from Iwakuni Air to Iwakuni Air Detachment at Naha, Takao; Info: Kure, Bako and U/I unit Takao. Indications are that 3rdFlt units are under way in a movement southward coordinated with 2ndFlt, Combined AF, and SEF.
S	24 Nov	Increased activity among 3rdFlt addressees with a high percentage of movement reports. Large number of messages associate CarDiv3 with CINC3. No definite location for carriers.
C	24 Nov	OPNAV message warning of possible Japanese "aggressive movement ... in any direction." Mentions Philippines and Guam as possible objectives.
S	25 Nov	High level of traffic suggests that organizational arrangements or other preparations are not yet complete. Genzan Air Corps has been in Saigon for eight days, according to callsign analysis. Other units of Combined Air Force possibly moved to French Indochina area from Taiwan. One or more CarDivs in Marshalls now.
S	26 Nov	CruDiv7 of Combined Fleet received traffic via Sama indicating arrival in Hainan waters, probably accompanied by DesRon3. *Takao*, former Flagship 2ndFlt active in association with 2nd/3rdFlts. No movement of

Flags newly formed force noted as yet. CINC5 association with new Task Force.

C   26 Nov   COM-14 260110Nov41 to OPNAV, Info: CINCPAC, CINCAF, COM-16; "JAPANESE NAVY ORGANIZATION OF FLEETS Submitted by the 14th Naval District Communication Intelligence Unit: Since the latter part of October, the Commander-in-Chief of the Second fleet has been forming a Task Force consisting of Second Fleet, Third Fleet (including First and Second Base Forces, and First Defense Division), Destroyer Squadron Three, Submarine Squadron Five, Combined Air Force Air Squadron Seven. Possibly vessels of the Third Battleship Division in the First Fleet. Third Fleet units are believed to be moving in the direction of Takao and Bako. It appears that the Seventh Cruiser Division and the Third Destroyer Squadron are an advance unit and may be en route to South China. The Combined Air Force has assembled in Takao, and indications are that some of it has already moved to Hainan Island. It seems that the Second Base Force is transporting equipment of the Air Force to Taiwan. Radio calls for the South China Fleet, the French Indochina Force, and the naval stations at Sama, Bako, and Takao appear also in headings of dispatches concerning this task force. The Resident Naval Officer, Palao, and the Third Base Force at Palao have communicated extensively with the Commander-in-Chief of the Third Fleet. It is thought that a strong force of submarines and air groups are in the vicinity of the Marshall Islands. This force includes the 24th Air Squadron, at least one aircraft carrier, and probably one third of the submarine fleet. The 14th Naval District Communications Intelligence Unit evaluates the foregoing information to indicate that a strong force may be preparing to operate in Southeastern Asia while component parts of the Task Force may operate from the Marshalls and Palao."

M   26 Nov   Pearl Harbor Strike Force departs Kuriles.

C   27 Nov   COM-16 261331Nov41, to CINCPAC, COM-14, OPNAV, CINCAF; "JAPANESE NAVY-ORGANIZATION OF FLEETS Date of Issue-27 November 1941. Following has been submitted by the 16th Naval District Communications Intelligence Unit, referring to and commenting on yesterday's information from the 14th Naval District Communications Unit. During the past few days traffic analysis indicates that the Commander-in-Chief, Second Fleet, is directing units of the First, Second, and Third Fleets, and Submarine Force organization that apparently will be divided into two sections. For purposes of clarity the units expected to operate in South China will be referred to as First Section and units expected to operate in the Mandates will be referred to as Second Section. The estimated units in First Section are Cruiser Division Seven, Air Squadron Six, Defense Division One, Destroyer Squadron Three, and Submarine Squadron Six. The Second Section consists of Cruiser Division Five, Carrier Division Three, (Ryujo and one Maru), Destroyer Squadrons Two and Four, Submarine Squadron Five, Destroyer Division twenty three, First Base Force of Third Fleet, Third Base Force at Palao, Fifth Base Force at Saipan, and lesser units unidentified. Cruiser Division Six and Battleship Division Three may be included in First and Second Sections respectively, but status cannot be clarified yet. There are slight indications today that Destroyer Squadron Three, Cruiser Division Seven, and Submarine Squadron Six are in the Takao area.   The balance of Third Fleet units in doubt but may be assumed that these vessels including Destroyer Squadron Five will take stations in the Straits of Formosa or further south. Combined Air Force units from the Empire proper are in Paidoh. [Possibly Paiho in South Central Taiwan.] It is impossible to confirm the supposition of reference report that carriers and submarines are in the Mandates. The best indications are that all known First and Second Fleet carriers are still in Sasebo-Kure area. Directives to the above Task Forces, if such, are directed to individual units and not to complete groups. Special calls usually precede formation of Task Force used in area operations. Commanders-in-Chief, Second, Third, and Southern Expeditionary Fleet, appear to have major roles. Traffic from the Minister of the Navy and the Chief of Naval General Staff to Commanders-in-Chief of the Fleet appears normal. This evaluation is considered reliable."

S   27 Nov   Some tactical traffic from carriers intercepted. DF activity high. No evidence of movement Combined Fleet from Kure/Sasebo area. Carriers still located in home waters.

C   27 Nov   OPNAV WAR WARNING message alerts all Pacific commands to "An aggressive move . . . within the next few days." Possible objectives mentioned: Philippines, Kra Peninsula, Thailand, or Borneo. Guam and Samoa to take measures against sabotage.

C   28 Nov   Naval attaché, Shanghai, on 25 November sights troop transports heading southwest; on 26 November, sights warships led by cruiser, possibly *Naka* [2ndFlt] heading south. Also reports that between 19 and 26 November, he had sighted many transports, many loaded with troops, headed southwest.

S   28 Nov   Communications volume between South China, Mandates, and Empire very heavy. No tactical traffic seen. Suspected "RI" net very active and becoming more so. DF and RI nets operating at full strength upon U.S. naval communications and getting results. In the Combined Fleet, no indications of any movement any Fleet units. In 3rdFlt, 1stBasFor possibly not in Sasebo but en route somewhere. In 4thFlt area, 4thBasFor at Truk, Yokohama Air Corps at Ruotto, and Wotje in communications with AirRon24 and Kamoi.

C   29 Nov   OPNAV WAR WARNING message. Text indicates Army also received warning. (290110Nov 41)

C   29 Nov   COM-16 reports CINC2 to move south between 29 November and 2 December. [291029Nov 41]

S	29 Nov	Traffic volume above normal. Traffic to South China very high. Intelligence-related messages numerous, e.g., 11 from Tokyo to Majcoms. Tokyo Radio Intelligence sent four long messages to Majcoms. DF net very active. Existence of 11thAirFlt confirmed. Not a Navy element. Arrival of AirRon7 in Takao confirmed. Following units under immediate command of CINC2: CarDiv3, DesRon2, SubRon5, DesRon4, SubRon6, 3rdFlt, CruDiv5, SEF, CruDiv7, and possibly two battleships subordinate to 3rdFlt.
C	30 Nov	OPNAV directs CINCAF to reconnoiter line from Manila to Cam Ranh Bay for evidence of Japanese preparations to attack Kra peninsula.
S	30 Nov	Traffic volume low; old messages being repeated. AKAGI (CV) heard on tactical circuit. Naval General Staff sent one urgent precedence message to COS Combined, 2nd/3rd/4th/5thFlts; Combined AF; Subs and China Fleets. In the Combined Fleet, COS, Combined and 1stFlts in Kure, COS2 is unlocated, possibly at sea. CINC2 addresses message to *Kongo* (BB) and *Hiyei* (BB) which places them in his Task Force. CINC3 possibly underway. 4thFlt area: CdrSubs headed for Marshalls. Evidence points to sub concentration [COM-16 disagrees]. Presence of AirRon24 and Yokohama Air suggests future Air/Sub operation from Marshalls. Presence of plane guard DDs suggests at least one carrier in Mandates.
C	1 Dec	COM-16 reports ships from 3rdFlt arriving Formosa. Notes CINC2 in Flagship *Atago* has moved south.
S	1 Dec	All radio calls of units afloat changed at midnight. Unusual. Service calls usually last six months. Suggests an additional progressive step in preparing for active operations on a large scale. 1stFlt: nothing to indicate Fleet out of home waters. Believe most of 1stFlt is in 2ndFlt Task Force. 2ndFlt believed proceeding from Kure/Sasebo in direction of South China, Indochina, probably passing up Takao. CruDiv7 and DesRon3 definitely in Indochina area. 3rd/4th/5thFlts NTR, Carriers, NTR; Combined Air Force, NTR. Large number of subs believed east of Yokosuka/Chichi Jima and Saipan.
S	2 Dec	COM-14/COM-16 disagree on precise location of 2nd/3rdFlt Task Force. COM-16 places in Takao area in communications with Takao radio. COM-14 did not hear but did note Takao sending traffic to Tokyo for these fleets suggesting they are not near Takao. Both seem to agree that the large fleet has left Empire waters. COM-16 reports nine subs vicinity Cam Ranh Bay, possibly SubRons5/6 which have been included in 2ndFlt Task Force. Possible that Combined Fleet staff has split, part to 2nd/3rd Flts, part elsewhere. 2ndFlt believed under way in company. 3rdFlt NTR. Carriers, almost complete blank. Traffic at low ebb. Not one callsign recovered. Some units of Combined AF have left Takao area.

C	3 Dec	OPNAV reports Japanese diplomats burning codes.
S	3 Dec	2nd/3rdFlts probably under way. Subs and carriers, NTR.
C	4 Dec	OPNAV orders certain U.S. intercept sites to burn codes.
M	4 Dec	Malay invasion force departs Hainan.
S	4 Dec	Tokyo sends large number [12] of urgent precedence messages to Majcoms. Intelligence sent seven-part message to COS China Flt, Combined Fleet, 3rdFlt, South China Flt, SEF, and Sama. CINC2 and CINC3 very quiet but receiving much traffic. CINC2 in vicinity of Takao. Cinc Combined sent message to U/I; Info: 3rdBasFor, Palao, CINC2, and CINC3.
S	5 Dec	All circuits overloaded. Tokyo-Mandates circuit duplex. Many new schedules. Both Takao and Tokyo handling traffic for 2nd/3rd Flts, some of which is old traffic. A plaintext message from a ship's captain from Tokyo to Takao referring to the Far Eastern crisis, notes that "specific orders will be issued soon." No traffic from Cdr carriers or sub force seen. In the 3rdFlt, a "COS" sent a message to "Commander 14th Army" aboard *Ryujo* Maru in 3rdFlt. A number of Maru vessels have been addressing CINC3. Shiogama Air and 2 U/I Corps are moving to probably Indochina.
C	5 Dec	Diplomatic message from Manila to Tokyo on 28 November details U.S. air patrols.
C	6 Dec	Diplomatic message from Honolulu to Tokyo on 18 November details ship movements in Pearl Harbor.
S	6 Dec	Traffic volume heavy but much old traffic seen. Much confusion in routing/delivery. Four stations now holding broadcasts: Tokyo [3] Saipan, Ominato, and Takao. CINC4 in Truk area, never in Jaluit. Definite close association between 3rdBasFor, Palao and forces in South China, e.g., 2nd, 3rdFlts, SEF, and Bako. Arrangements largely neglected by CINC4. 5thFlt dispersed in Empire waters.

Notes

1. For many years communications intelligence was also known in the Navy as traffic intelligence if derived from traffic analysis and radio intelligence when derived from decrypted messages.

2. Since 1912, when Admiral George Dewey, chairman of the General Board, decreed that military men should limit themselves to "purely military questions," U.S. Navy war planners did not consider either domestic or foreign motives for war. This situation prevailed until at least the 1960s. Ronald Spector, *Professors of War: The Naval War College and the Development of the Naval Profession* (Newport, R.I.: Naval War College Press, 1977). Cryptography is the development of codes and ciphers; cryptanalysis is the exploitation of codes and ciphers.

3. 18 August 1917 memorandum from Radio Officer to the Commanding Officer, Series II.E.6, Center for Cryptologic History (CCH) History Collection.

4. Notes and Comments on the Necessity for and the Organization of a Cipher Bureau, 1918; A summary of the Organization, Activities, and Achievements of the Code and Cipher Section of the Military Intelligence Division (MI8), November 1918, by Chief Yeoman H. E. Burt, USN, Series II.E.62 and II.E.63, CCH History Collection (classified).

5. *The Birthday of the Naval Security Group* SRH-150; Record Group 457, Records of the National Security Agency, National Archives; hereafter RG 457, NA; a series of declassified ONI memorandums involving Chief Radioman (CRM) H. A. Williams on 12, 15, and 16 April 1924 and 17 July 1924 clearly show their interest in the quality of intercept material supplied by Station A. ONI no doubt would inform the Chief of Naval Operations if anything of naval or national interest was learned from the messages. Chief Williams was stationed at Shanghai at the time. Series II.E.36, CCH History Collection; Jeffrey M. Dorwart, *Conflict Of Duty, The U.S. Navy's Intelligence Dilemma,* 1919–1945 (Annapolis, MD: Naval Institute Press,1983), 41–42.

6. Jack S. Holtwick, Captain, USN (Ret), unpublished manuscript, "Naval Security Group History to World War II," SRH-355, 67, RG 457, NA; anecdote about Navy Slush Fund and establishment of Research Desk was taken from Captain Laurance F. Safford, unpublished manuscript, "The Undeclared War, History of RI," SRH-305, RG 457, NA. For a biographic background of Hooper, see L. S. Howeth, Captain, USN (Ret), "History of Communications Electronics in the U.S. Navy," (Washington, D.C.: Government Printing Office, 1963), in which he is called the father of naval radio.

7. SRH-355, 45–48. RG 457, NA.

8. Ibid., 52.

9. Dedication of the memorial to the "On the Roof Gang," Series III.H.26; Interview Duane L. Whitlock, Captain, USN (Ret), 11 February 1983, by Robert Farley, OH-05-83, NSA (classified).

10. 13 May 1929 memo from CNO to CINCAF, Appendix A, SRH-180., RG 457, NA.

11. SRH-355, 223, footnote. RG 457, NA.

12. COM-13 correspondence with OP-20 in July and August 1930, Series II.H17, CCH History Collection (classified).

13. 22 May 1932 letter from CNO to Rear Admiral E. H. Campbell, COM-13, Series III.H.17, CCH History Collection (classified); see also SRH-355, 67, RG 457, NA.

14. 22 March 1932 memorandum to COM-13 from CNO, Series III.H.17, CCH History Collection (classified) and 27 April 1932 memo same to same, Series III.H.17.1, CCH History Collection (classified); see also SRH-355, 67, RG 457 NA.

15. Interview John H. Gelineau, CWO, USN (Ret), 4 October 1983, by Robert Farley, OH-22-83, NSA (classified).

16. 11 June 1931 memorandum CNO to COM-14, Series III.H.17, CCH History Collection (classified). Without explaining what "unofficial intercept activities" meant, CNO ordered the station "reestablished."

17. Navy records for December 1941 show the following dispositions: Collection – Total number of receivers, 68: Guam–9; Corregidor–25; Heeia–21; Bainbridge Island (formerly Astoria)–13, SRH-197 "U.S. Navy Communication Intelligence Organization, Liaison and Collaboration, 1941–1945," RG 457, NA; see also SRH-355, 243–44, RG 457, NA.

18. SRH-355, 50–51. RG 457, NA.

19. Memorandum from CINC U.S. Fleet to Chief of Naval Operations dated 15 May 1929, Series III.H.1, CCH History Collection (classified).

20. 10 May 1930 letter Safford to Dyer, Series III.H.10.3, CCH History Collection.

21. SRH-355, 391. RG 457, NA.

22. U.S. Fleet Problems X and XI, Series III.H.10.3, CCH History Collection.

23. Part IV, Communications, in "Command Conclusions on U.S. Fleet Problem 9," Series III.H.1, CCH History Collection (classified). This is a very brief paraphrase of the paragraph on radio security.

24. SRH-355, 155. RG 457, NA.

25. SRH-222, 223, 224, 225, RG 457, NA. Various reports on Japanese Grand Fleet maneuvers 1930, 1933, 1934, 1935.

26. SRH-355, 131, RG 457 NA; see also Gordon Prange with Donald M. Goldstein and Katherine V. Dillon, *The Verdict of History* (New York: McGraw-Hill, 1986), 134. On 4 November 1941, an OPNAV message reported this fact to CINCPAC, CINCAF, and others. See also Safford, SRH-305, 20. RG 457, NA.

27. SRH-355, 118–119, RG 457, NA.

28. Ibid., 222–223, RG 457, NA.

29. Ibid.

30. Captain Laurance F. Safford, unpublished manuscript, "A Brief History of Communications Intelligence in the United States," SRH-149, RG 457, NA.

31. History of Signal Security Agency, Series III.hh, CCH History Collection (classified).

32. Herbert O. Yardley, *The American Black Chamber*, originally published in book form 1 June 1931.

33. 29 October 1931 memorandum from DNC to CNO via DNI, "Allocation of RI Activities Between the Army and the Navy," Series VII.19, Box 4, Vol. 1, pre-1942, CCH History Collection (classified).

34. 29 October 1931 memorandum from OP-20-G to CNO via DNI, Series VII.19, Box 4, Vol. 1, CCH History Collection (classified).

35. 12 April 1933 memorandum for the Director of Naval Communications from J. W. McClaran, OP-20-G, Series VII.19, Box 4, Vol. 1, CCH History Collection (classified).

36. There is no record of this episode in the Department of State files.

37. RG 220, NA. Proceedings of the Joint Board, National Archives, Joint Board Memorandum, 24 April 1933.

38. A series of unclassified memoranda between CNO, the Joint Board, and the Secretary of War during the period March–July 1933, Joint Board #319, Serial 516. RG 220, NA.

39. Interview Prescott H. Currier, Captain USN (Ret), 14 November 1980, by Robert Farley and Henry Schorreck, OH 39-80 (classified).

40. SRH-149. SRH-305, RG 457, NA.

41. OP-20-G memorandum Serial 051220 dated 25 July 1940, "Coordination of Intercept and Decrypting Activities of the Army and Navy," Series VII.18, Box 4, 19, CCH History Collection (classified).

42. See 14 February 1946 memorandum for OP-20-4 from Captain L. F. Safford, "Responsibility for Decoding and Translating Japanese Intercepts," Series VII, Box 4, 19, CCH History Collection (classified).

43. "History of JNA 20" (CORAL), Vol. I. NSA Cryptologic Archival Holding Area (classified).

44. SRH-305, RG 457, NA and SRH-149. RG 457, NA.

45. This code was stolen without the knowledge of the Japanese soon after its introduction in 1939. "History of OP-20-GYP," 2, Series IV.W.I.5.12, CCH History Collection (classified).

46. "History of OP-20-3-GYP," 2. Series IV.W.I.5.12, CCH History Collection (classified).

47. Ibid.

48. Ibid.

49. "Military Study Communication Intelligence Research Activities," United States Navy, 30 June 1937, SRH-151, RG 457, NA.

50. History of OP-20-GYP-1, Series IV.W.I.5.13, CCH History Collection (classified).

51. SRH-149, RG 457, NA; see also 7 December 1929 memorandum to DNI from DNC, "Radio Intelligence." At that time the main purpose of the Research Desk was deciphering Japanese codes, Series III.G.9, CCH History Collection; Japanese traffic volumes, Howe monograph, *Early Background of the U.S. Cryptologic Community*, Series VII.15, CCH History Collection; Army-Navy DOE, 1931, Navy proposed to divide diplomatic communications based on availability of intercept and Naval power, Series VII.19, Box 4, Vol. I pre-1942, CCH History Collection (classified); Japanese Blue Book introduced February 1931, SRH-305, RG 457, NA.

52. "History of OP-20-GYP-1," Series IV.W.I.5.13, CCH History Collection. See also Edwin T. Layton, *And I Was There*, (New York: William Morrow and Co., 1985), 77.

53. "History of OP-20-GYP-1," Series IV.W.I.5.13, CCH History Collection (classified).

54. Ibid.

55. Ibid.; see also Layton, *And I Was There*, 77-78, 249.

56. Ibid.; see also "History of OP-20-GY Series IV.W.I.5.10 – 12:13, CCH History Collection (classified).

57. "History of OP-20-GYP-1" (classified).

58. Interview Frank B. Rowlett, 26 November 1974, by Vincent Wilson, Henry Schorreck, David Goodman and Earl Coates, OH-01-74, NSA (classified).

59. Ibid.

60. Friedman monograph *Preliminary Historical Report on Solution of the B Machine*, 14 October 1940, Series IV.I.2.28, CCH History Collection (classified).

61. SRH-305, RG 457, NA.

62. Part of OP-20-G's workload is described in SRH-149, RG 457, NA and SRH-305, RG 457, NA. See also the history of OP-20-GY, Series IV.W.I.5.10, CCH History Collection (classified).

63. *History of Signal Security Agency*, Vol. III (classified), contains a copy of appropriate portions of the act, Series III.hh. See also W. J. Holmes, *Double-Edged Secrets* (New York: Berkley Books, 1981), 13-14, which states that this act prohibited a commercial radio company in Honolulu in early 1941 from sharing daily Japanese ship position data inherent in commercial weather messages with COM-14's intelligence collection effort.

64. Prange, *Verdict of History*, 7.

65. H. P. Willmott, *Empires in the Balance* (Annapolis, MD: Naval Institute Press, 1982), 30-51. The actual ratios: battleships and heavy cruisers, 5.5.3; light cruisers and destroyers, 10.10.7; and submarines, 1.1.1. See also Prange, *Verdict of History*, 7. By standing aloof from the League of Nations, the U.S. had rejected collective security, yet it had refused to provide for itself an adequate unilateral national defense system. Prange also asserts a weak argument supported by several quotations that blame for Pearl Harbor actually lay with the American people who, because of complacency, idealism and a false sense of security based on racial arguments, failed to insist that Congress provide for adequate military strength after World War I.

66. "U.S. Naval Pre-World War II Radio Intelligence Activities in the Philippine Islands, 1931–1942," SRH-180, RG 457, NA.

67. SRH-355, 421, and Appendix VII, 289-90. The linguist in at least one instance was also head of the Diplomatic section in Station C.

68. Ibid., 311. RG 457, NA.

69. Interview, Thomas H. Dyer, Captain, USN (Ret) January-March 1982, by Robert Farley, OH-01-82, CCH, and NSA interview Rudolph T. Fabian, Captain, USN (Ret) 4 May 1983 by Robert Farley OH-09-83, CCH (classified). Hereafter Dyer interview, Fabian interview.

70. SRH-355, 167–168. RG 457, NA.

71. Dyer interview.

72. Dyer interview; interview Wesley A. Wright, Captain, USN (Ret), 24 May 1982, by Robert Farley and Henry Schorreck, OH-11-82, CCH; interview Edwin T. Layton, February 1983, by Robert Farley, OH-02-83, CCH.

73. SRH-355, 330–331. RG 457, NA.

74. Ibid., 218–222 . RG 457, NA.

75. Military Study, SRH-151. RG 457, NA.

76. Asiatic (1), Mid Pacific (2), West Coast (3), Cavite–18*, Heeia–17*, Astoria–7, Guam–10*, Shanghai–7, Augusta–1, (*includes 2 for HFDF). East Coast-U.S. Fleet (4), East-West Coast DF (5), Winter Harbor–7, CINCUS–10, Navy Dept.–2, Students–8, Total 87. "A Military Study of the Radio Intelligence Organization," June 1937, Series IV.W.X.11, CCH History Collection (classified).

77. Cavite, a minor research center, 6; Flagship Asiatic Fleet, an advanced mobile unit, 3; Flagship U.S. Fleet, a mobile unit, 4; Pearl Harbor, a major research unit, 5; and Washington, a major research unit, 25, including administrative personnel. Ibid.

78. On 3 July 1940, the COMINT unit aboard the USS *Trenton* was transferred to the USS *Omaha* in Squadron 40T and began covering Italian naval circuits in the Mediterranean. Naval battles between Italian and British forces during July and August and the attack on Rhodes in September 1940 were reported by this unit. SRH-355, 372. RG 457, NA.

79. The material in this section concerning U.S. strategic planning is based on several sources: "War Plan Orange: Evolution of Strategy," Lewis Morton, World Politics, January 1959, 221–250; "Naval Contingency War Plans 1891–1945," Scholarly Resources, Wilmington Delaware, 1979; "The U.S. Navy: Strategy, Defense and Foreign Policy 1932–1941," Michael Kedian Doyle, Ph.D. dissertation, University of Washington, 1977, University Microfilm International, Ann Arbor, MI, and London; "The U.S. Navy and War Plan Orange 1933–1940: Making Necessity a Virtue," Michael K. Doyle, Naval War College Review, May–June 1980; and "Strategic Planning for Coalition Warfare 1941–1942," Maurice Matloff and Edwin M. Snell, Office of the Chief of Military History, Dept of the Army, Washington, D.C., 1953.

80. "Professors of War: The Naval War College and the Development of the Naval Profession," Ronald Spector (Newport, RI: Naval War College Press, 1977), 71-2, 108–111.

81. Both Laurence Safford and A/CNO RADM Royal E. Ingersoll indicated (Pearl Harbor Attack Hearings Before the Joint Committee on the Investigation of the Pearl Harbor Attack, Congress of the United States, 79th Congress, hereafter PHA, part 26, 388 and part 9, 4241, respectively) in their testimonies that they believed Hawaii was responsible to CINCPAC; Safford in his testimony to the Hart inquiry, Ingersoll while being cross-examined by Kimmel during the congressional investigation. It was Safford, of course, who in 1937 opened the office, assigned Dyer and others to COM-14, and allocated all cryptanalytic tasks until 1942.

82. Memorandum from CNO to COM-14, 21 August 1937, "Cryptanalysis, Orange M1 System" Series III.H.17, CCH History Collection (classified). The M-1 was a Kana cipher machine used by the Japanese Navy from July 1933 for about four years. It is described in RIP28. Jack S. Holtwick, *A Guide to Foreign Cryptographic Systems: U.S. Navy Short Titles, Cover Names, and Nicknames*, 14 June 1971. NSA Cryptologic Archival Holding Area (classified).

83. 14 February 1938 memorandum CNO to COM-14, "Hawaiian Decrypting Unit, Equipment and Personnel for," Series III.H.17 CCH History Collection (classified).

84. Prange, *Verdict of History*, 212. CNO, Admiral Stark, was committed to the Germany-first strategy, and he hoped to ward off conflict with Japan as long as possible.

85. SRH-355, 368–370. RG 457, NA. See also Prange, *Verdict of History*, 400, where Bloch is shown as not understanding his COMINT unit as a source of information on Japanese fleet activities when he told General Short that such information came from Washington. In addition, Prange also attributes to Captain Ellis M. Zacharias, USN, ONI that Bloch was antagonistic toward intelligence (possibly just toward Zacharias) and that Kimmel should have either replaced Bloch or corrected the problem.

86. SRH-355, 370. RG 457, NA.

87. SRH-355, 402. RG 457, NA.

88. Radio Intelligence Publications (RIP) No. 39 and 51, SRMN 069 and 072, RG 457, NA..

89. SRH-355, 223, 248, 260 RG 457, NA; NSA interview David Snyder, CWO, USN (Ret), 3 October 1983 by Robert Farley, OH-21-83, (classified); "History of OP-20-GYP-1" Series W.I.5.13, CCH History Collection (classified).

90. See also SRH-180. RG 457, NA U.S. Naval Pre-WWII RI Activities series.

91. Appendix A, Study of Intercept Activities 23 Aug 1940, Revised 27 September 1940, Series VII, Box 4, Vol. I, pre-1942, CCH History Collection (classified).

92. Howeth, 543.

93. "History of OP-20-GYP-1," Series IV.W.I.5.13, CCH History Collection (classified), and SRH-355, 420. RG 457, NA.

94. Snyder interview (classified); Currier interview (classified). SRH-355, 420–21. RG 457, NA.

95. SRH-355, 420–21. RG 457, NA.

96. NSA interview, Thomas H. Dyer, Captain USN (Ret) Jan-Mar 1982 by Robert Farley, OH-01-82 CCH

97. SRH-355, 316–17, 394, 351, RG 457, NA. A letter from Nimitz to Halsey on 28 Oct 1942 which indicates that even at that date, motorcycles were still used for carrying traffic from Wahiawa to Pearl Harbor, Series IV.Q.5.5, CCH History Collection.

98. Morison, Vol. III, 42–43; NSA interview, Thomas H. Dyer, OH-01-82; Edwin T. Layton, *And I Was There*, 51.

99. See Appendix C in toto and "Combat Intelligence Unit, 14th Naval District," TI Summaries with comments by CINCPAC War Plans and Fleet Intelligence." SRMN-012, RG 457, NA. See also Prange, *Verdict of History*, 453–43, which cites Kimmel's testimony at the congressional hearings when he said he had no reason to suspect the six missing carriers had been converted into a "lost fleet" during November. In fact, before the 17 November procedure change it was clear that these carriers had been assigned to a separate organization, the 1st Air Fleet. (See Appendix A.) However, neither COM-16 nor Layton picked this up as an important development though it was reported by COM-14 on 6 November. See appendix C. See also "Notes on Communications Security," prepared by J. R. Dennis, 17 November 1942, Series IV.W.I.5.8, CCH History Collection (classified).

100. *Intelligence Reports by Pacific Fleet Intelligence Officer*, PHA, part 17, 2643.

101. See appendix C and SRMN-012: COM-14 Daily Comint Summaries for 16 July, 31 July, 28 September, 2 October, 16 October, 21 October, 22 October, 23 October, 6 November, 21 November, 29 November, and 2 December. See also footnote 1 in Prange, *Verdict of History*, 446, which refers to Kimmel's testimony before Congress (Part 6 beginning on p. 249). Clearly reflecting Layton's assessment of traffic analysis and D/F as sources, Kimmel describes information thus derived as "open to serious doubts" unless supported by readable messages. Examples cited show how closely he was following T/A reports from both COM-14 and COM-16, however.

102. Whitlock interview (classified) and Appendix C.

103. P.H.A. Part 14, 1405, item 33.

104. Considering that Station C belonged to the 16th Naval District, it may seem a bit unusual for CNO to use the CINCAF channel without reference to COM-16. The 16th Naval District, however, was a problem district/command. It was subordinate to CINCAF, but after 1939 the Navy had trouble keeping the commandant's position filled. Between 1939 and 1941, three men, Rear Admiral John M. Smeallie, Rear Admiral Harold M. Bemis, and Rear Admiral Francis W. Rockwell, were appointed. It was not uncommon, as the Japanese crisis grew more intense, to see communications such as this concerning Station C passing directly from Washington to Hart, bypassing COM-16 entirely.

105. Morison, Vol. III, 71.

106. John B. Lundstrom, *The First South Pacific Campaign; Pacific Fleet Strategy December 1941- June 1942* (Annapolis, MD: Naval Institute Press) 8–11. [See also Mitsuo Fuchida and Masatake Okumiya, *Midway, the Battle that Doomed Japan*, Annapolis, MD: U.S. Naval Institute, , 1955), 48 and following.]

109. Ibid.

110. H. P. Willmott, *Empire in the Balance* (Annapolis, MD: Naval Institute Press, 1982) 80-82.

111. Morison, Vol. III, 161.

112. Morison, Vol. III, 87.

113. Appendix C concerns the movements of Japanese navy, air and military units of the Southern forces. Its contents were extracted from daily reports between July and December 1941 prepared by the COMINT unit in Hawaii which drew on intercept from Heeia as well as reports from Corregidor. The abundant detail of these reports contrasts sharply with the histories written of the period such as Morison's Vol. III, *Rising Sun in the Pacific*, because historians such as Morison did not have access to this type of record. The purpose of preparing Appendix C is to show the value of COMINT as a source of indications, intentions, order of battle, and warning, even when the underlying messages cannot be exploited.

114. OP-20-GT-P, the traffic analysis section in Washington, was not established until early 1942.

115. Ibid.

116. Gordon Prange, *At Dawn We Slept*, (New York: McGraw-Hill, 1981), 326–33; on or about 5 November 1941, Combined Fleet Operations Order #1, revealed Pearl Harbor as the Strike Force objective; SRN-117687, RG 457, NA, this message imposes radio silence on 6th Fleet submarines on 11 November 1941; SRN-116866, RG 457, NA, this message shows that radio silence was imposed on the entire Combined Fleet on 26 November 1941.

117. See Appendix A. See also Prange, *At Dawn We Slept*, chapter 40, 320–25, and *Verdict of History*, chapter 25, which discuss Japanese efforts to modify torpedoes and Kimmel's conviction that torpedoes could not run in the shallow waters of Pearl Harbor after being launched from a plane. Had he seen these messages he would no doubt have changed his mind.

118. See message of 4 November 1941, Appendix A.

119. SRN-117453, 116476, 117301, and 116323, RG 457, NA. See also Prange, *At Dawn We Slept*, chapter 40, 320–25.

120. SRN-117453, 116684, 117301, 116323, 117665, 115709, 115784, RG 457, NA.

121. SRN-116239/116901, 115709, 116588, 116131, 116583, RG 457, NA.

122. Morison, Vol. III, 89.

123. Ibid.

124. SRN-115787. RG 457, NA.

125. SRN-115375. 117683. RG 457, NA.

126. SRN-115787. RG 457, NA.

127. SRN-117673, 117674/117666, 116990/116329, 116436, 116643, 116920, RG 457, NA. See also Prange, *At Dawn We Slept*, 342–52.

128. SRN-116588, RG 457, NA.

129. See Appendix A.

130. See Appendix A.

131. Connorton, Vol I.

132. See Appendix C, where all the OPNAV warning messages of November 1941 are shown in the specific context of the COMINT summaries from Hawaii and indirectly from Corregidor. See also PHA, part 10, 4834, in which Layton asserts his conviction that the two messages in fact stimulated the war warning from CNO on 29 November.

133. See Appendix B. In preparing Appendix B, I have selected certain Japanese diplomatic messages intercepted and translated between July and 6 December 1941. The messages were usually seen by authorized recipients on the day they were translated. Army and Navy translations are shown in juxtaposition with the warning messages issued by the Chief of Naval Operations using the heading OPNAV.

134. Roberta Wohlstetter, *Pearl Harbor, Warning and Decision* (Stanford, CA: Stanford University Press, 1962).

135. Wohlstetter, 176–86.

136. See Wohlstetter, 221 and 227, for example, and see Appendix B. See in particular the message translated on 4 December from Rome to Washington.

137. Ibid.

138. Connorton, Vol. I.

139. See Appendix A.

140. James Leutze, *A Different Kind of Victory* (Annapolis, MD: Naval Institute Press, 1981), 198–230.

141. See Appendix C.

142. Morison, Vol. III, 151.

143. Leutze, *A Different Kind of Victory*, 226.

144. Thomas C. Hart, *Narrative of Events, Asiatic Fleet*, a personal diary (Washington, D. C.: Naval Historical Archives).

145. Leutze, *A Different Kind of Victory*, 226.

146. Hart, *Narrative of Events, Asiatic Fleet*

147. SRN-117284, 116772, 117290, RG 457, NA.

148. SRN-116645, 116647, 116729/116730, RG 457, NA.

149. Leutze, *A Different Kind of Victory*, 222, and Commander Walter Karig and Lieutenant Welbourne Kelley, *Battle Report, Pearl Harbor to Coral Sea*, (New York: Farra and Rinehart, Inc.,1944), 129–130.

150. SRN-117284, 116772, 117290, RG 457, NA.

151. Tentative chronology/memorandum for the record dated 3 August 1944 from OP-20-G, NMCG, subject: "Assignment of Washington on Various Naval Systems during the Year 1941," found in Rochefort papers, Series IV.W.X.1.a, CCH History Collection (classified).

152. OP-20-G was completely reorganized in February 1942, though not along the lines recommended by Safford. On 5 March 1942, COM-16 was directed by CINC to "evacuate personnel of Radio Intelligence unit as soon as possible."

Abbreviations Used in Text and Appendixes

Adm	Admiral
Addees	Addresses
ALNAV	All Navy
AirRon	Air Squadron
A/CNO	Assistant Chief of Naval Operations
BatDiv	Battleship Division
BB	Battleship
BasFor	Base Force
Bdcst	Broadcast
CA	Heavy Cruiser
C/A	Cryptanalysis
CarDiv	Carrier Division
Cdr	Commander
CINCAF	Commander in Chief, Asiatic Fleet
CINCPAC	Commander in Chief, Pacific Fleet
CINC2	Commander in Chief, Second Fleet
CL	Light Cruiser
CNO	Chief of Naval Operations, OPNAV
Coll	Collective
COMINT	Communications Intelligence
COMSEC	Communications Security
COM-16	Commandant, 16th Naval District
ComCarDiv	Commander, Carrier Division
ComUnit	Communications Unit
COS	Chief of Staff
COSCombined	Chief of Staff Combined Fleet
COS2	Chief of Staff, Second Fleet
CruDiv	Cruiser Division
CV	Fleet Carrier
CVL	Light Carrier
DD	Destroyer
DesRon	Destroyer Squadron
DF	Direction Finding
DNC	Director of Naval Communications (OP-20)
DNI	Director of Naval Intelligence (OP-16)
DOE	Division of Effort
FECB	Far East Combined Bureau
1st AirFltStf	First Air Fleet Staff
1stSecCh	First Section Chief
Flt	Fleet
GC&CS	Government Code and Cipher School
GD	Guard District
GdDiv	Guard Division
Hydro	Hydrographic
InfBde	Infantry Brigade
InfDiv	Infantry Division
Majcom	Major Command
MI	Military Intelligence

MilPrep	Military Preparations
Msgs	Messages
NavalAux	Naval Auxiliaries
NavalSec	Naval Section
ND	Naval District
NGS	Naval General Staff
NTR	Nothing to Report
OIC	Officer in Charge
ONI	Office of Naval Intelligence
OPNAV	Chief of Naval Operations
Orange	Japan
OTRG	On the Roof Gang
PBY	Amphibious Patrol aircraft
P.H.	Pearl Harbor
RCA	Radio Corporation of America
R/Adm	Rear Admiral
Reg't Grp	Regimental Group
RI	Radio Intelligence
RIP	Registered Intelligence Publication
RNO	Resident Naval Officer
Scty	Secretary
SECNAV	Secretary of the Navy
SEF	Southern Expeditionary Force
6FLT	Sixth Fleet
SIGINT	Signals Intelligence
SRH	Special Research Histories
SS	Submarine
T/A	Traffic Analysis
Tech Bur	Technical Bureau
Tfc	Traffic
T/I	Traffic Intelligence
Tokyo Comms	Tokyo Communications Unit
UK	United Kingdom
VAdm	Vice Admiral
Yrd	Yard

ꭓ

Notes on Sources

Primary Sources

The NSA History Collection consists of manuscripts, memoranda, studies, and interviews related directly or indirectly to the cryptologic history of the United States. The extensive records in Series III (1919–39), Series IV, pertaining to the years of World War II, and Series VII, a special series, upon which I have drawn for my research were collected by former NSA Historian Henry F. Schorreck.

Also included within the files of the history program are important special collections of personal papers including those of William F. Friedman and Carter W. Clarke. These collections, however, have remained intact apart from the index system and have their own finding aids.

Other archival collections which have also proved invaluable are the National Security Agency Cryptologic Archives, Ft. George Meade, Md.; the Classified Naval Archives, Washington Navy Yard, Washington, D.C.; the Roosevelt Library, Hyde Park, New York; the Naval Security Group Repository, Federal Records Center, Naval Weapons Supply Center, Crane, Indiana; the U.S. Naval Academy Library; and of course the National Archives, Washington, D.C., which houses Record Group (RG) 457, the NSA collection. I would like to make special acknowledgment to Brian von Swearingen, the Naval Security Group Historian, for his courtesy and his enthusiastic support in obtaining records of OP-20-G from Crane; to the personnel at the Naval Academy Library for their help in locating obscure works in their extensive collection on the history of naval planning and access to their invaluable microfiche records of the Orange Rainbow plans; and to the assistance of the historian at the Classified Naval Archives for alerting me to the Hart diary and to the records of Orange Rainbow and other prewar planning initiatives taken by the U.S. Navy.

Of the million or more pages of documentation supplied the National Archives by NSA, I have drawn extensively on the following series as they pertain to Japanese matters: the SRH series containing narrative materials pertaining to cryptologic history; the SRN series, which consists of individual translations of Japanese Navy messages; and the SRMN series, which represents discrete records of historical cryptologic impact originated by the U.S. Navy. All of this material can be found in RG 457.

Within the body of these records, after the translations of Japanese Navy messages (SRN series), two publications stand above all others: SRH-012, John V. Connorton's effort on Japanese diplomatic messages, which is Volume I of his monumental work entitled "The Role of Radio Intelligence in the American-Japanese Naval War," published in 1943, and SRMN-012, the Combat Intelligence Unit, 14th Naval District Traffic Intelligence Summaries, published daily after 16 July 1941, with comments by CINCPAC Fleet Intelligence and CINCPAC War Plans.

Finally, it should be apparent that some of my material concerning cryptologic operations in Hawaii and the Philippines has been drawn from personal experiences. For this I am indebted to the NSA Oral History (OH) program administered by the late Mr. Robert Farley. Copies of all interviews cited are located at NSA.

Secondary Sources

The noncryptologic elements of this chapter in COMINT history necessarily drew on the perspective of many others, from diarists to distinguished historians, to reconstruct plausible cause and effect relationships between historical and cryptologic developments. Since the result is, I believe, a unique view, particularly of the final months of 1941, made possible by heretofore unexamined material, I must take full responsibility for its conclusions.

Two of the military service official histories were very useful. The official Navy history was of significant and continuing value. Samuel Eliot Morison's *History of U.S. Naval Operations in World War II* provided invaluable perspective on world disarmament and Japanese relations with China, as well as precise details on Japanese Navy and Army order of battle in the western Pacific on 7–8 December 1941. Of necessarily lesser importance in what is essentially a Navy-oriented history, but still valuable, is Louis Morton's treatment of Japanese preparations for war and opening strategy in the *U.S. Army in World War II, The War in the Pacific,* and *Strategy and Command: The First Two Years,* which also provided the inspiration for some of my illustrations.

In addition to many fine American authors such as Gordon Prange, Edwin Layton, Clay Blair, Jr., Jeffrey Dorwart, and James Leutze, the biographer of Admiral Thomas C. Hart, to name but a few, I also benefited immensely from the work of two English authors, H. P. Willmott and Christopher Thorne. Their books, *Empires in the Balance* and *Allies of a Kind,* respectively, provided profound commentary on Japanese motives, aspirations, and planning.

Two other secondary sources deserve separate and special mention. Almost before the fires were extinguished at Pearl Harbor, the executive branch of the U.S. government, as well as the Navy and the Army, had launched investigations into this terrible disaster. All of the reports generated by this activity were consolidated into a single, massive, thirty-nine-volume (plus appendixes) report of the 79th Congress entitled "Pearl Harbor Attack, Hearings before the Joint Committee on the Investigation of the Pearl Harbor Attack." Cited herein as PHA, such material was most valuable in preparing this history. For the period before the war, I am equally indebted to an unpublished manuscript prepared by the late Jack S. Holtwick, Captain, USN (Ret), entitled "Naval Security Group History to World War II." This manuscript, which has been turned over to the National Archives, would have been listed as a primary source if all the documents uncovered by Holtwick could be examined by other historians.

Two sources which I could not locate would have added significantly to this history: Corregidor's records, which were probably burned, and records from Washington which discuss the relationship between OP-20-G, ONI, and War Plans during the days before Pearl Harbor. Despite their obvious value and importance to this story, I doubt if anything will ever again match the satisfaction of finding in Gordon Prange's book *At Dawn We Slept* the name of Lieutenant Commander Suguru Suzuki, who had been a Japanese spy at Pearl Harbor until early November 1941. The satisfaction came because I had already encountered his name in messages on 18 and 19 November 1941, as he was being transported to Hittokapu Bay probably to deliver his report.

I would like to thank all the members of the former History and Publications Division, particularly Henry F. Schorreck and Gerald K. Haines, for their encouragement, guidance, and timely criticism in the construction of this history. They overcame my initial misgivings about preparing still another history of this period and convinced me that the Agency's archives contained unique and undiscovered treasures.

Bibliography

Primary Sources

SRH 045 – Reminiscences of Harold W. Brown 1932 – August 1945.

SRH 355 – Naval Security Group History to World War II, Jack S. Holtwick.

SRH 151 – Military Study Communications Intelligence Research Activities, U.S. Navy, 30 June 1937, Joseph N. Wenger.

SRH 305 – The Undeclared War – History of Radio Intelligence 1943, Captain L. F. Safford, USN.

SRH 149 – A Brief History of Comint in the U.S. – 1952, Captain L. F. Safford, USN.

SRH 159 – Preliminary Historical Report on Solution of the "B" Machine, 14 October 1940 (Purple).

SRH 161 – Permanent Organization for Code and Cipher Investigation and Attack (1916–19).

SRH 179 – History of Station A.

SRH 020 – History of JICPOA, W. J. Holmes.

SRH 233 – Lessons Learned from Pearl Harbor.

SRH 255 – Interview of Robert D. Ogg (Seaman Z).

SRH 222, 223, 224, 225 – Reports on Imperial Fleet Maneuvers.

SRH 150 – The Birthday of the Naval Security Group.

SRH 154 – SI Disclosures in the Pearl Harbor Investigation.

SRH 012 – The Role of Radio Intelligence in the American-Japanese Naval War, August 1941 – June 1942, John V. Connorton, Lieutenant j.g., USNR.

SRMN 012 – 14th Naval District TI Summaries with Comments by CINCPAC War Plans and Fleet Intelligence, 16 July 1941 – 30 June 1942.

SRN – Individual Translations proposed 1945–46.
  115202 – 116365, October – December 1941.
  116366 – 117412, June – December 1941.
  117413 – 117616, September – December 1941.
  117617 – 117840, September – December 1941.

James B. Captron. Interview, NSA OH-25-84.

John E. (Vince) Chamberlin. Interview, NSA OH-15-84.

Prescott Currier, Captain, USN (Ret). Interview, NSA OH-02-72.

Thomas H. Dyer, Captain, USN (Ret). Interview, (Naval Institute) NSA OH-1-6-83.

Thomas H. Dyer, Captain, USN (Ret). Interview, NSA OH-1-82.

Rudolph T. Fabian, Captain, USN (Ret). Interview, NSA OH-9-83.

John Gelinean. Interview, NSA OH-22-83.

E. S. L. Goodwin, Captain, USN (Ret). Interview, NSA OH-4-83.

Frank B. Rowlett. Interview, NSA OH-01-74 to NSA OH-14-81.

David W. Snyder, CWO, USN (Ret). Interview, NSA OH-21-83.

John H. Tiltman, Brigadier, British Army. Interview, NSA OH-01-79.

Duane L. Whitlock, Captain, USN (Ret). Interview, NSA OH-05-83.

Wesley A. (Ham) Wright, Captain, USN (Ret). Interview, NSA OH-11-82.

Secondary Sources

Andrew, Christopher,and David Dilks, eds., *The Missing Dimension – Governments and Intelligence Communities in the 20th Century*. Urbana: University of Illinois Press, 1984.

ASA Historical Background, Vol. III.

Bacon, Reginald, and Francis E. McMurtrie, *Modern Naval Strategy*. Brooklyn, New York, 1941.

Ball, Desmond J. *Allied Intelligence Cooperation Involving Australia During World War II, Australian Outlook: Journal of the Australian Institute of International Affairs* (1978), 32:3.

Blair, Clay. *Silent Victory*. Philadelphia and New York: J. B. Lippincott, 1975.

Conway's All the World's Fighting Ships 1922–1946. New York: Mayflower Books, 1986.

Corson, William P. *The Armies of Ignorance – The Rise of the American Intelligence Empire*. New York: Dial Press, 1977.

Dorwart, Jeffrey M. *Conflict of Duty* (1945–46). Annapolis, Maryland: Naval Institute Press, 1983.

Doyle, Michael Kedian. "The U.S. Navy: Strategy, Defense, and Foreign Policy" Ph.D. dissertation, Ann Arbor, Michigan: University Microfilms International and London, 1977.

_____. "The U.S. Navy and War Plan Orange 1933–1940: Making Necessity a Virtue." *Naval War College Review*, May–June 1980, 49.

Dyer, Vice Admiral George C.USN (Ret.). *The Amphibians Came to Conquer, The Story of Admiral Richmond Kelly Turner*, Vol. I. Washington, D.C.: GPO, 1969.

Farago, Ladislaw. *The Broken Seal*. New York: Random House, 1967.

Freedman, Lawrence. "Intelligence Operations in the Falklands." *Intelligence and National Security*, Vol. 5 (September 1986), No. 3, 311–312.

Fuchida and Okumiya, *Attack on Pearl Harbor*, 2nd ed. Annapolis, Maryland: U.S. Naval Institute, 1971.

Fukudome, Shegeru, Rear Admiral, Japanese Imperial Navy, *Hawaii Operation* (Japanese official title for Pearl Harbor attack), 2nd edition. Annapolis, Maryland: U.S. Naval Institute Press, 1971. Originally published in *Proceedings*, this is an anthology.

Harris, William R. A biography with selected annotations in *Intelligence and National Security*, 1968.

Hart, Admiral Thomas C.,USN, A personal diary covering 8 December 1941 and period immediately before. Hart was CINCAF at the time.

Horner, D. M. *Australian Outlook: Journal of the Australian Institute of International Affairs*, Vol. 32:3, 1978.

Hough, Richard. *The Greatest Crusade – Roosevelt, Churchill and the Naval Wars*. New York: William Morrow and Company, Inc., 1986.

Howeth, L. S. *History of Communications and Electronics in the U.S. Navy*, Washington, D.C.: GPO, 1963.

Japanese Navy in World War II, an anthology based on articles which appeared in *Proceedings*.

Japanese Black Chamber, Series IVZ.10.2, CCH History Collection

Kazuo, Sakahami. *I Attacked Pearl Harbor*. The perspective of a commander of a midget sub.

Kelley, Welbourne, and Walter Karig, *The Story of Patwing 2 in the Philippines*, Battle Report, Pearl Harbor to Coral Sea.

Kent, Sherman. *Strategic Intelligence for American World Policy*. Princeton, New Jersey: Princeton University Press, 1949.

Kimball, Warren E. *Churchill/Roosevelt Correspondence*, Vol. I. Princeton, New Jersey: Princeton University Press, 1984.

Laquer, Walter. *A World of Secrets – The Uses and Limits of Intelligence*. Basic Books, 1985.

Layton, Rear Admiral Edwin T. USN (Ret.). *And I Was There*. New York: William Morrow and Company, Inc., 1985.

Leutze, James. *A Different Kind of Victory*. A biography of Thomas C. Hart, Admiral, USN. Annapolis, Maryland: Naval Institute Press, 1981.

Lowenthal, Mark M. *U.S. Intelligence: Evolution and Anatomy*, Georgetown University CSIS. New York: Praeger, 1984.

May, Earnest R.,ed. *Knowing One's Enemies – Intelligence Assessment Before the Two World Wars*. Princeton, New Jersey: Princeton University Press, 1984.

Maurer, Alfred C., Marion D. Tunstall, and James M. Keagle, eds., *Intelligence: Policy and Process*. Boulder and London: Westview Press, 1984.

The Battle of Midway (U.S. Naval War College, 1948), Series IV WXI.14., CCH History Collection.

Morison, Samuel Eliot. *History of U.S. Navy in World War II*, Vol. 1; *The Rising Sun in the Pacific, 1931 – April 1942*, Vol III. Boston: Little Brown and Co., 1975.

Prange, Gordon. *Pearl Harbor, The Verdict of History*. New York: McGraw-Hill, 1986.

_____. *At Dawn We Slept*. New York: McGraw-Hill, 1981.

Spector, Ronald. *Professors of War: The Naval War College and the Development of the Naval Profession*. Newport, Rhode Island: Naval War College Press, 1977.

Stevens, William O. "Scrapping Mahan," *Yale Review*, 12 April 1923, 528–42.

Thorne, Christopher. *Allies of a Kind*. New York: Oxford University Press, 1978.

Toland, John. *Infamy, Pearl Harbor and its Aftermath*. Garden City, New York: Doubleday & Co., Inc., 1982.

U.S. Congress. Pearl Harbor Attack, Hearings Before the Joint Committee on the Investigation of the Pearl Harbor Attack. 79th Cong.

VanDerRhoer, Edward. *Deadly Magic*. New York: Charles Scribner & Sons, 1978.

Willmott, H. P. *Empires in the Balance, 1921–1941*. Annapolis, Maryland: Naval Institute Press, 1982.

Wohlstetter, Roberta. *Pearl Harbor Warning and Decision*. Stanford, California: Stanford University Press, 1962.

Yardley, Herbert O. *The American Black Chamber*. Indianapolis: The Bobbs–Merrill Co., 1931.

Mr. Parker retired from NSA in 1984 after thirty-two years of service. Following his retirement, he worked as a reemployed annuitant and volunteer in the Center for Cryptologic History. Mr. Parker served in the U.S. Marine Corps from 1943 to 1945 and from 1950 to 1952. He holds a B.S. from the Georgetown University School of Foreign Service.

26189923R00060

Made in the USA
San Bernardino, CA
21 November 2015